OVERWORKED, UNDERPAID, UNSTOPPABLE

HOW TO LEAD, RISE, AND THRIVE IN DENTISTRY'S TOUGHEST ROLE

By Kyle L. Summerford

DEDICATION

For Jasmine—

for believing in me before I believed in myself.

This book, this journey, and this future—it's ours.

&

For every hardworking office manager

who has ever felt unseen, unheard, or unappreciated—

this is for you.

&

And for the younger version of me,

grinding through recall calls,

eating half a bagel for lunch,

and dreaming of something more—

you didn't quit.

You built something that matters.

CONTENTS

ACKNOWLEDGEMENTS

Mary—You were the guiding light and mentor I never knew I needed. You believed in me during my best moments and stood by me through my worst. You never made me feel small when I was struggling, and you never stopped pushing me to think bigger than I thought I could. This book exists, in no small part, because of who you were to me when I was just a kid trying to figure it all out. Thank you.

Dad—You were tough on me, and I am grateful for every single moment of it. You taught me that you must serve others before you can serve yourself—a value the military instilled in you and that you passed down without ever having to say it out loud. You were a man of uniform, a man of discipline, and a man of quiet strength. I carry that with me every day.

Mom—You ran our home like a command center and made it feel like a sanctuary. You chose to stay home and pour yourself into raising your children, and that choice shaped everything about who I became. The structure, the warmth, the consistency—that was all you. Thank you for nurturing us and for never letting the house feel like anything less than a home.

My brother—You taught me lessons the hard way, and I mean that with love. A knockout or two along the way taught me to be firm, to stand my ground, and to follow through even when it was uncomfortable. You were tough because life is tough, and you prepared me for it better than you probably know.

Hailey, Kyle Jr., and Juliette—Everything I have built, I have built with you in mind. You are the reason this book exists beyond just a story—it is a blueprint I hope you carry with you.

I want you to see in these pages the same values, the same work ethic, and the same belief in something bigger than yourself that I had to learn the hard way. If this book gives you even one shortcut around the hard lessons I had to go through, then it was worth every late night and every word. I love you more than anything I have ever built.

To my DOMA members and everyone who read my articles, shared my strategies, and followed Dental Coding with Kyle—You were there before the stages, before the community grew into what it is today, before any of this felt possible. You read my words when I was still finding my voice. You shared my lessons when I was still learning them myself. You showed up consistently and reminded me that what I had to say actually mattered. This book is yours as much as it is mine.

And to every dental office manager who has ever felt overworked, underpaid, and invisible—this was written for you. You are seen. You are valued. And you are more unstoppable than you know.

PROLOGUE: YOUR BACKGROUND IS YOUR BOOTCAMP

We didn't have it all, but we had enough to know better.
That made all the difference.

I was born in the '80s and raised in the '90s, back when phones had cords and dinner happened at the same table every night. We weren't poor, but we weren't floating either. We sat in that tight space between the low and middle classes, where you had what you needed, but every dollar had a job.

I had one brother. Just us, side-by-side in a household that ran on structure, effort, and discipline. My dad served in the Air Force during the Vietnam War as a helicopter pilot. After the military, he worked for the U.S. Postal Service, and after retiring from the post office, he still couldn't sit still, so he volunteered with the NYPD Auxiliary. He was quiet but steady.

My mom didn't work outside the house, but make no mistake—she worked. Her full-time job was running that household. She cooked every day. Dinner was always on the table, even if it was instant mashed potatoes and canned vegetables. That kitchen was her command center. She may not have clocked in, but the way she ran that house would put most managers to shame.

⏣ Manager Musings

"If you want to understand operational efficiency, don't shadow a CEO. Watch a stay-at-home mom cook three meals a day on a tight budget while keeping everyone fed, clean, and out of trouble."

We weren't a family that sat around talking about feelings. But everything was modeled. My dad didn't preach work ethic—he showed it. Every Sunday morning, you'd find him at the table, reading the paper, clipping coupons with a precision that rivaled dental charting. He'd organize them into stacks, plan the week, and make sure we got every bit of value out of that grocery budget.

My mom, on the other hand, brought structure and predictability. Chores weren't negotiable. Meals were planned. And even if we had the same three side dishes on rotation, there was comfort in knowing what to expect. She made a home out of hard work, not fancy things.

That foundation—the quiet commitment, the reliable rhythm—is the exact kind of energy I bring into the offices I manage today. When everything's falling apart, when the staff is at each other's throats, when the schedule looks like Swiss cheese, I don't panic. I remember that kitchen table. I remember problems being puzzles, not catastrophes.

That mindset didn't come from nowhere—it came from the era I grew up in. The '90s were different. Growing up in that time built a particular kind of awareness. A grit that you don't learn from textbooks.

We played outside until dark. There was no DoorDash, no Amazon Prime. You learned how to wait. You learned how to hustle. And if something was broken, you either fixed it or learned to live without it. That mindset would later shape how I handled broken dental chairs, failed software rollouts, and cranky patients. You can always find a way.

Dinner was our daily meeting. It wasn't fancy. It wasn't always peaceful. But it was sacred. Plates clinked. Stories got told. Plans got made. That table taught me about resourcefulness and accountability. If we were low on something, we figured it out.

That sense of self-sufficiency stuck with me. It shows up in the way I troubleshoot at work, train my teams, and step up when nobody else will. I'm not afraid of a challenge, because I was raised to create solutions—not wait for them. We weren't handed things, but we were handed values. Show up. Do your best. Don't make excuses. Be reliable—even if no one's watching. That's what I carried into adulthood.

🧠 *Manager Musings*

"A leader isn't born in a boardroom. Sometimes, they're born in a small kitchen with mismatched plates, a coupon-clipping dad, and a mom who never let a dinner burn—even when everything else felt like it might."

THE JUMP: FROM SURVIVAL TO SERVICE

Before I ever entered a dental office, I was just a kid trying to figure out how to build a life—and fast.

By eighteen, I was married. By nineteen, I had a child on the way. I wasn't thinking about careers; I was thinking about how to survive. I bounced between a few jobs—retail mostly. Gap Kids was one of them, folding tiny denim jackets and wondering how I was going to make ends meet. I knew I needed a more stable and serious type of work, something that offered a clearer career path and could support my new family.

That's when I ended up in a dental lab. Not because I had a passion for dentistry, but because I needed a paycheck and I was willing to learn. That job wasn't glamorous—but it gave me a window into an industry I had never considered.

I wasn't clinical. I wasn't technical. But I noticed how much organization, timing, communication, and detail it took just to get one crown out the door. Eventually, I started connecting the dots. And soon after, I made a leap that would change everything—I took a job doing recalls in a dental office. And that's where this story really begins.

But the truth is, it all started with the values I learned back at home. From my dad, who showed up every day for his family, clipped coupons to stretch every dollar, and believed in serving something bigger than himself. From my mom, who kept the household running with love, leftovers, and lessons I didn't realize I'd carry into every room I'd one day lead.

This book may be about what happened after I got into dentistry, but who I became started long before that. And over the next twenty chapters, I'm going to show you exactly how to take wherever you came from—whatever your concrete beginnings—and turn them into your competitive advantage.

YOU'LL DISCOVER THE HARD-WON WISDOM FROM THE TRENCHES:

- How to master the dreaded recall list and turn cold calls into conversions
- The exact moment I shifted from staff to leader, and how you'll recognize yours
- How I took an office no one wanted and turned it into a top performer
- Why a practice turnaround became my business school

YOU'LL LEARN FRAMEWORKS THAT ACTUALLY WORK:

- The power of the morning huddle to transform your team's energy and productivity
- How to scale yourself without burning out
- Why managing people isn't about managing tasks—it's about managing energy and expectations
- The Bagel Method™—yes, it involves actual bagels, and yes, it will revolutionize how you present treatment

YOU'LL HEAR ABOUT MY FAILURES (SO YOU CAN AVOID THEM):

- The broken promise that taught me more than any success

- Why I had to testify in court, and what it taught me about trust

- The burnout that almost broke me, the boundaries that saved me, and getting fired for doing what was right

YOU'LL SEE THE TRANSFORMATION POSSIBLE:

- Building a practice that could run without me—the ultimate test of leadership

- From dental office manager to community builder—creating the Dental Office Managers Community (DOMA) and finding my tribe

- From the back office to the keynote stage—saying yes before I felt ready

- Creating a career that wasn't handed to me—and how you can, too

This isn't a textbook. It's not theory from someone with an MBA who's never sat in your chair. This is battlefield medicine—practical, proven strategies from someone who's been in the trenches, made the mistakes, and figured out what actually works.

If you're feeling overworked, underpaid, and invisible right now, I need you to know: I was you. Every struggle you're facing, every doubt you're fighting, every ceiling you're hitting—I've been there. And I'm going to show you exactly how to break through.

But it all starts with understanding that your background isn't your baggage—it's your bootcamp. Those recall calls you're avoiding? That's where you'll learn persistence. That toxic office environment you're surviving? That's where you'll learn how to create culture. That burnout you're fighting? That's where you'll learn boundaries.

Next up, in Chapter 1, I'll take you into the recall trenches and show you how doing what others won't do becomes your secret weapon.

JOURNAL PROMPT

What's one lesson from your upbringing that still guides your leadership style today? Was it something someone said—or something they simply showed you? Write it down. Because that lesson—those roots—will be more important than you think as we build your leadership story together.

CHAPTER 1

STARTING AT THE BOTTOM

Some people find their calling. Others start on a landline, doing the dirty work no one wants— and end up leading the whole thing.

Every dental office has that stack of names, gathering dust—the overdue patients who haven't been in for six months, a year, or sometimes longer. I'm sure you already know what I'm talking about: the dreaded recall list.

Most practices treat recalls like a punishment duty—something to dump on the newest hire while everyone else finds "urgent" filing in another room. But here's what twenty years in this industry has taught me: the recall list is the single best training ground for everything you'll need to succeed as a dental office manager.

Master the recall list, and you learn the fundamentals of practice management. Avoid it, and you miss the education that no course can provide.

DOING WHAT OTHERS WON'T

The cramped back office where I started smelled like stale coffee and copy toner. My desk had barely enough room for my elbows, and my weapon of choice was a phone that felt like it weighed as much as a brick—the clunky, corded kind that clicked when you hung it up too hard.

My mission? Cold calls. One after another. Day in, day out. I wasn't smiling and dialing for stock picks, but it felt a lot like that "Wolf of Wall Street" grind. I was Jordan Belfort—but for dental recalls.

"Hi, this is Kyle calling from Dr. So-and-So's office. I noticed you're overdue for your cleaning—can we get you back on the schedule?"

Eight hours a day, two days a week, dialing through lists of overdue patients. Countless dials. Countless rejections. But within those calls, I discovered something: the recall list teaches you three critical skills that determine your success as a manager:

SKILL #1: READING PEOPLE THROUGH THEIR VOICE ALONE

Within three seconds of someone answering, you know exactly where you stand. The sharp "What?" tells you they're defensive. The apologetic "Oh, hi..." means they know they're overdue and feel guilty. The cheerful "Hello!" suggests they're open but need a reminder of why dental care matters.

I learned to read voices like poker tells. The apologetic tone meant guilt about staying away. The defensive edge signaled a bad experience. The hesitation usually meant money troubles. Each voice taught me something about human nature, about fear, about trust.

This skill—instantly reading emotional states and responding appropriately—becomes invaluable when you're managing staff conflicts, handling patient complaints, negotiating with vendors, or navigating difficult conversations with doctors.

SKILL #2: TURNING REJECTION INTO INTELLIGENCE

Most people see rejection as failure. But every "no" on the recall list is actually free market research.

"I can't afford it" tells you something about your payment options. "I don't have time" reveals something about your scheduling. "I'm scared" shows you what your marketing should address. "I had a bad experience" teaches you what to fix in your patient experience.

Start tracking the actual reasons people give for not scheduling. After a hundred calls, you'll see patterns that reveal exactly what your practice needs to improve. This strategy can provide the same type of intelligence gathering that companies pay thousands for in focus groups—and you're getting it for free.

SKILL #3: PROFESSIONAL PERSISTENCE WITHOUT BEING A PEST

Here's what I discovered about recall success: It's rarely about the first call. It's about becoming a pleasant, consistent presence in someone's awareness until they're ready.

Some patients need three touches before they'll schedule. Others need six. The key is staying professional and positive without making them feel guilty. I learned to leave voicemails that made people smile instead of cringe. To send reminders that felt personal, not automated.

The average practice loses 15–20% of patients annually, but half aren't really gone—they're just procrastinating. Master friendly persistence, and you recover thousands in lost production. That patient who finally schedules after your fourth touch? They don't just bring their $200 cleaning. They bring their $2,000 crown, their family's treatment, their referrals. One recovered patient can mean $10,000 in lifetime value.

This skill transfers everywhere—getting insurance claims paid, getting doctors to complete notes, getting staff to follow through. It's the difference between asking once and hoping, versus professionally persisting and actually getting results.

> ⊛ *Manager Musings*
>
> *"The work you do when no one's watching? That's what qualifies you to lead when everyone is."*

BROKE, TIRED, BUT ALL IN

Let me paint you a picture of what "all in" really looked like for me.

I'd wake up at 5 AM to embark on a grueling commute from Astoria, Queens, to Bayside—two trains, two buses, and a 15-minute walk—for a two-day-a-week, minimum-wage position cold-calling patients for overdue cleanings. I'd buy one bagel in the morning and eat half for breakfast, saving the other half for lunch. Yep, you read that right: a single bagel was my daily food budget.

While the rest of the team ordered lunch together, I'd quietly eat my half-bagel at my desk, pretending I wasn't hungry for more. In truth, I was hungry, but not in the way you'd expect—I was hungry to learn, hungry to grow, and hungry for opportunity.

MARY: MORE THAN A MANAGER

Mary was our office manager, but she was also the heartbeat of the practice. She noticed things, like how I never ordered lunch with the team. She never made it awkward. When she noticed I wasn't eating enough, she'd casually leave "extra" lunch on my desk. "Can't finish all this, Kyle," she'd tell me. No production, no pity. Just quiet care that let me keep my dignity while making sure I was fed.

One day, Mary pulled me aside. "The doctors want to try something," she said. "For every ten patients you get scheduled, they'll give you twenty dollars. Cash."

Twenty dollars. To someone who needed to support a family and was making minimum wage, that was a proposition I couldn't turn down. More than that, it was recognition that this work—the work everyone else ran from—had real, measurable value.

That bonus lit something in me. I kept a tally sheet next to my phone, marking off every scheduled appointment. Ten marks meant twenty dollars, but it also meant ten people getting care, ten relationships rebuilt, ten small victories that proved the system worked.

Mary fought for my raises before I knew how to fight for myself. She pulled me into meetings I had no business being in—yet. She was playing a long game, and I was her investment.

THE SILENT DENTISTS

The doctors who owned the practice—two brothers—barely spoke to the team. They were silent, stoic, and always watching—studies in contrast to Mary's warmth. They'd walk through the office like ghosts, present but not really there. Months could pass with nothing more than a "Morning" or a nod. It may not have been the healthiest practice culture, but that silence did teach me an important lesson: work speaks louder than your words ever can.

I knew they were watching. They saw me show up early, stay late, and grind through call lists no one else would touch. They noticed when I figured out problems on my own. They observed how I handled difficult patients, frustrated staff, and system failures.

I realized that their silence wasn't indifference—it was evaluation. And when they needed someone they could trust, they remembered who did the work without being asked. All of that grinding taught me more than persistence—it taught me process.

LESSONS FROM THE RECALL TRENCHES

Those thousands of calls taught me more than any business school could. Here's a "Recall System Action Plan" I developed in the trenches:

Phase 1: Set the Foundation (Days 1–10)

- Clean your data—remove deceased patients, moved patients, and explicit opt-outs
- Create tracking sheets for rejection reasons
- Set realistic daily goals (quality over quantity)
- Document your current scripts and success rate as a baseline

Phase 2: Develop Your Approach (Days 11–20)

- Practice reading voice tones in the first three seconds
- Test different opening lines until you find what works
- Focus on building relationships, not just booking appointments
- Track which approaches get the best response

Phase 3: Build Your System (Days 21–30)

- Create voicemail scripts that make people smile
- Develop a follow-up timeline (initial call, voicemail, text if permitted, mailed reminder)
- Train someone else on what works
- Calculate the actual revenue impact of your improved system

The Metrics That Matter:

- Conversation rate (how many dials become actual conversations)
- Scheduling rate (how many conversations become appointments)
- Show rate (how many scheduled actually appear)
- Production value (treatment identified through recall appointments)

FROM RECALL CALLS TO REAL LEADERSHIP

Mary saw something in me during those grinding days—not just someone willing to do the dirty work, but someone who could transform it into something valuable. When she fought for my raises and pulled me into responsibilities I had no business being in yet, she wasn't just promoting a recall specialist. She was betting on someone who'd proven they could take the job nobody wanted and build something from it.

That bet was about to pay off.

Next, in Chapter 2, I'll share how I went from the back office to the front desk, and why moving up meant learning that you can't be everyone's friend anymore.

What "dirty work" in your practice are you avoiding that could become your competitive advantage? List three unglamorous tasks that, if mastered, could transform your value to the practice.

FROM PEER TO BOSS

Sometimes growth doesn't look like a promotion—it looks like a moment when someone believes in you before you believe in yourself.

After months of crushing it on recalls—scheduling 400 to 500 patients monthly, turning every ten scheduled patients into twenty dollars cash—I noticed something troubling. Our office couldn't keep a front desk receptionist. That position was cursed—turnover after turnover, each person lasting just weeks or months before disappearing.

Finally, I worked up the courage to ask Mary: "Can I do it? Can I be the front desk receptionist?"

She didn't even hesitate. She marched upstairs to the older brother's office. Next thing I knew, I was standing in front of him as he asked me if I thought I could ask people for money or if I'd have a problem with that. Without missing a beat, I told him I knew I could, and I'd do it well.

Suddenly, I wasn't hidden in the back anymore. I was front and center, face-to-face with patients, responsible for scheduling, payments, phone calls, and follow-through.

THE SHIFT FROM STAFF TO LEADER

Moving to the front desk wasn't just a position change; it was a career shift. More than that, it was the beginning of my transformation from worker to leader. Through this journey, I discovered there are three distinct stages every new leader must navigate. Miss one, and you'll struggle indefinitely.

THE THREE STAGES OF LEADERSHIP EVOLUTION

Stage 1: The Competence Test

Can you do the job better than anyone else?

At the front desk, I started taking on more responsibility. Not because anyone asked, but because problems needed solving. Billing questions, patient issues, doctor requests, small fires that could become wildfires. I didn't have a title, but I had something more valuable: trust.

This is where most aspiring leaders get stuck. They think doing more work equals leadership. But competence is just the entry fee. The real test comes next.

Stage 2: The Conflict Test

Can you handle difficult conversations without running away?

It wasn't long before I faced my first real team conflict. Two coworkers couldn't get along. Passive aggression turned into eye-rolls and side comments. It finally boiled over with me caught in the middle.

I could've walked away. Let Mary handle it. That's what the old me would have done. But something inside told me to step up. So I addressed it, set boundaries, and created space for real conversation.

It wasn't perfect—far from it. But it was a turning point. That day, I learned leadership isn't just about keeping things moving, but knowing when to stop everything and address what's festering underneath.

Stage 3: The Character Test

Can you own your mistakes without losing your authority?

Here's the part most leadership books skip: You're going to screw up. Publicly. Painfully. And how you handle it determines whether your team will follow you or just comply.

There were times I scheduled patients for the wrong treatment—had them show up expecting one thing, only for the doctor to pull up the chart and give me that look. There were other times I flat-out forgot to enter appointments. The patient would walk through the door, cheerful and on time—and there'd be no record of them anywhere.

That moment? When you realize you're the reason they weren't scheduled? It hits hard. I'd have to step into the operatory, interrupt the doctor, and say, "Hey... this one's on me."

Then I'd wait—hoping he'd still see them and not make me be the one to break the bad news.

But the one that haunted me most? Overcharging patients. Not malicious—just me, still learning, pulling from the wrong fee schedule or miscalculating copays. Then having to call that patient, admit the mistake, and explain a refund was coming. Awkward. Humbling.

I became obsessed with accuracy after that. Double-checking everything. Creating verification systems. My mistake became our office's strength.

LEADERSHIP ISN'T JUST DOING—IT'S DECIDING

The more competent I became, the more decisions landed on my desk. Small ones at first—which vendor to use, how to handle a scheduling conflict, whether to squeeze in an emergency patient.

But then bigger decisions came. Staff conflicts that needed resolution. System changes that affected everyone. Patient complaints that could damage our reputation.

THE DECISION FRAMEWORK THAT SAVED MY SANITY

I developed a simple system for making decisions without drowning in them:

For Immediate Decisions:

- Will this matter in 24 hours? If no, make a quick call and move on

- Will someone be harmed by waiting? If no, it can wait

- Do I have 70% of the info needed? If yes, decide now

For Team Decisions:

- Who will this affect? Include them in the discussion
- What's the worst-case scenario? Plan for it
- What's reversible vs. permanent? Start with reversible

For Major Decisions:

- Sleep on it (but only one night)
- Get input from someone outside the situation
- Consider the precedent it sets
- Document the reasoning for future reference

BALANCING BURNOUT AND GROWTH

Even in these early days, I could feel the weight of trying to be everything to everyone. The two-hour commute each way. The constant pressure to perform. The growing responsibilities without growing pay.

Life outside the office didn't pause for my professional growth. I was dealing with the realities of a young marriage under strain, raising a child, and managing bills that always seemed bigger than the paycheck.

There were many nights I got home running on fumes, when I missed putting my daughter to bed, left wondering if this path was even worth it. But I kept going. Because for the first time, I wasn't just surviving—I was becoming something. I was learning not just what we did, but why it mattered.

Looking back, the seeds of burnout were already being planted. I didn't recognize these as warning signs then. I thought they were just the price of success. I'd learn later how wrong I was.

ASKING FOR THE NEXT BIG STEP

After five years at this first practice—five years of recalls, front desk, taking on more responsibility—I knew I was ready for more. I'd learned everything I could from Mary. I'd proven myself to the silent brothers. I'd made every mistake there was to make and learned from each one.

The brothers had purchased a second location in Oakland Gardens, Queens, a few years earlier. Now, it was struggling, and the previous manager had just given notice. The practice was hemorrhaging money and morale. Seizing the opportunity, I caught the older brother in a rare moment of availability.

"I want the opportunity to manage the Oakland Gardens office," I said.

He paused. Looked at me for what felt like forever. Then gave a quiet nod. "We'll try it," he said. "Start Monday."

That was it. No fanfare. No congratulations. Just an opportunity and an expectation.

Getting the go-ahead on Oakland Gardens brought mixed feelings. I was leaving the safety of what I knew—on my own, without Mary's daily guidance. But I carried every lesson with me: her leadership style, her toughness, her belief in people before they believed in themselves.

It was time to see if I could build something of my own. I was scared, excited, and completely unsure if I could pull it off. But you're never really ready. You just decide to try anyway.

Next, in Chapter 3, I'll share how I took the Oakland Gardens practice from failure to thriving, and what happens when you have to build trust from absolutely nothing.

JOURNAL PROMPT

What opportunity is presenting itself that scares you? What would you need to believe about yourself to say yes? Sometimes the biggest growth comes from the moments when we feel least prepared but step forward anyway.

TURNING A FAILING PRACTICE AROUND

Sometimes the biggest opportunity looks like a complete mess—and that's exactly where leaders are born.

There I was—Oakland Gardens, Queens. The place where everything changed.

On paper, this practice should have been thriving. Good location. Solid patient base. But walking in that first day, I could feel it—that heavy, oppressive air of a practice dying from the inside out. Production was around $300,000—way below potential. Morale was in the basement. Systems were nonexistent. The front desk staff barely looked up when I walked in. Patients were coming in, but they weren't coming back.

Five years had passed since I'd started making those recall calls. Five years of Mary's mentorship, of climbing from the back office to the front desk, of proving myself worthy of bigger challenges. Now the brothers had given me my shot: turn around their failing second location. No safety net. No Mary to lean on. Just me and a practice that nobody else wanted.

THE OFFICE NO ONE WANTED

The physical space itself was depressing. Flickering fluorescent lights that gave everyone headaches. Dental chairs with temperamental hydraulics that would randomly drop patients mid-procedure. Water-stained ceiling tiles from old leaks. The reception area furniture was worn and dated, magazines from two years ago scattered on scratched tables.

The team was even more broken than the furniture. Everyone worked in silos. The assistants ate lunch separately from the admin staff. Nobody talked in the hallways. The morning routine was everyone sneaking to their stations, avoiding eye contact, just trying to get through another day.

It was time to buckle up. This was the opportunity the brothers gave me—my chance to lead.

BUILDING TRUST FROM SCRATCH

The team didn't trust me at first. Why would they? To them, I was just another outsider from the main office, probably here to fire some folks, implement impossible new rules, and leave them to clean up the mess. But Mary taught me that trust isn't granted by title—it's earned through action. So, I took action.

I started with the basics nobody wanted to do—literally rolling up my sleeves and getting my hands dirty. I cleaned the bathroom. I took out the trash. I organized the supply closet that had become a dumping ground. When the hydraulic fluid started leaking from the dental chair—again—I got under there with towels and a wrench.

Now, let's be real—I wasn't a repair tech. There were times I absolutely made things worse. Like the time I tried to fix a broken bracket and ended up cracking the casing even more. But I never sat around waiting for someone else to fix it. I tried. I failed. And sometimes I pulled off a miracle.

I MacGyver'd plenty of things using whatever I had—alginate, acrylic, cotton rolls, you name it. It wasn't pretty, but it kept the day moving. The team saw me trying, failing, and trying again. They saw me show up at 6 AM to deal with problems before patients arrived. They saw me stay until 8 PM to help with insurance claims nobody understood.

Within three weeks, something shifted. The eye rolls stopped. The whispered conversations ended. People started coming to me with problems instead of hiding them.

SYSTEMS, STANDARDS, AND SOME PUSHBACK

Once I had a little trust, I could start implementing real change. But I'd learned from my mistakes at the first office—you can't change everything at once. So, I started with one thing: the morning huddle.

"We don't have time for meetings," they said. "This is pointless," they complained. "The last manager tried this and it didn't work," they warned.

But I kept it simple. Ten minutes. Every morning. Non-negotiable.

At first, it was painful. People showed up late, participated grudgingly, rolled their eyes through the whole thing. But I kept going. Every day. Same time. Same format. By day 30, something interesting happened. The team started showing up on time for the huddle. By day 60, they were contributing ideas. By day 90, they were running portions of it themselves.

THE POWER OF THE MORNING HUDDLE

The morning huddle had become our secret weapon at Oakland Gardens. But I kept evolving it, making it more powerful, more focused, more energizing.

Creating Your Power Huddle

The Energy Opener (Minutes 1–2)

Start with wins from yesterday. Any wins. A patient compliment. A perfect handoff. Energy builds from celebration, not criticism.

The Opportunity Review (Minutes 3–5)

Who's coming in today? What treatment is pending? What's our production goal? Frame everything as opportunity, not obligation.

The Obstacle Anticipation (Minutes 6–8)

What might go wrong? Who's running late? What insurance issues are pending? Anticipate to prevent, don't wait to react.

The Daily Challenge (Minutes 9–10)

One specific, measurable goal for today. Something everyone can impact. "Let's hit 90% case acceptance." "Zero gaps in the schedule."

Essential Rules:

- Start on time, always
- Everyone speaks at least once
- No problems without proposed solutions
- End with energy, not tasks

The magic wasn't just in the meeting itself. It was in what happened after. The team started communicating proactively. Problems got solved before they became crises. People started showing up differently—not just physically, but mentally.

REBUILDING TRUST—ONE CONVERSATION AT A TIME

The biggest challenge wasn't systems or schedules—it was the poisoned communication culture. Front desk versus back office. Clinical versus admin. Everyone versus everyone. So, I had individual conversations. Lots of them. I'd pull people aside—not in a confrontational way, but in a "help me understand" way.

"What's working for you here?"

"What makes your job harder than it needs to be?"

"If you could change one thing, what would it be?"

After dozens of these conversations, patterns emerged. Everyone felt unappreciated. Everyone felt overworked. Everyone felt like "those other people" didn't understand their challenges.

The breakthrough came when I started having people shadow each other. The front desk spent a day as an assistant.

Assistants worked the phones. The clinical team handled insurance verifications.

Suddenly, everyone understood why the front desk got stressed when rooms ran over. The front desk understood why assistants needed proper setup time. The walls between departments began to come down.

WHEN IT STARTED TO CLICK

The turning point wasn't dramatic. It was a random Thursday afternoon, about four months in.

I walked out of my office to find the team huddled together at the front desk. My first thought was "What's wrong now?" But as I got closer, I heard them problem-solving together. The schedule had imploded due to an emergency, and instead of panic and finger-pointing, they were figuring it out together.

The front desk was calling patients to reschedule. Assistants were resetting rooms for different procedures. The doctor was actually participating instead of hiding in his office. They didn't need me to solve it.

That's when I knew we'd turned the corner.

Over the next several months:

- Production went from $300,000 to over seven figures
- No-show rate dropped to under 10%
- Treatment acceptance increased to 75%
- Online reviews went from one star to four-plus
- Staff turnover stopped completely

But here's what really mattered: The team started smiling. Patients started referring friends. The oppressive air lifted. It became a place where people wanted to work, where patients wanted to come.

YOUR 90-DAY TURNAROUND BLUEPRINT

Days 1–30: Stabilize

- Implement one non-negotiable daily practice (like a morning huddle)
- Create simple tracking for your biggest problem area
- Fix the obvious physical issues (broken equipment, cleanliness)
- Listen more than you talk

Days 31–60: Build Foundation

- Develop basic protocols for common procedures
- Create accountability through visible metrics
- Start celebrating small wins publicly
- Begin cross-training for coverage

Days 61–90: Create Momentum

- Add more advanced tracking systems
- Identify and develop emerging leaders
- Document what's working
- Set growth goals based on your baseline

WORKING WITH CONSTRAINTS

Here's what nobody tells you about turnarounds: your most considerable constraints often force your best innovations.

We had newly graduated dentists who were still getting comfortable with handpieces. Simple procedures took forever. Root canals stretched to three hours and brought in just $200 from insurance.

We couldn't make procedures faster, but we could make them more valuable. While patients were in those lengthy appointments, we focused on relationship building. We learned about their families, their fears, their goals. Those three-hour root canals became three-hour relationship investments.

We couldn't compete on speed, so we competed on patient experience. We became known as the practice that never rushed you, that really listened, that made you feel like family. Our constraint became our differentiator.

> *"You don't need perfect providers. You need persistent processes. Build around what you've got, not what you wish you had."*

THE LESSONS OAKLAND GARDENS TAUGHT ME

That struggling practice became my real education. It taught me that trust is earned in the trenches, not granted by title. That systems don't have to be complex to be transformative. And that turning around a practice isn't about being the hero— it's about creating conditions where everyone can succeed.

But success has its own dangers. The better you get at solving problems, the more problems find you. The more indispensable you become, the less freedom you have. That's a lesson I was about to learn the hard way.

Oakland Gardens went from the practice nobody wanted to work at to the practice nobody wanted to leave. And once you prove you can fix one broken thing? Everyone wants you to fix their broken things too.

Next, in Chapter 4, I'll share how I learned to develop others while managing a crisis that could have destroyed everything we'd built—and why sometimes the hardest decisions are the ones that protect everyone.

What broken situation in your life could become your greatest teacher? What would change if you stopped seeing it as a problem and started seeing it as your opportunity to prove what you're capable of?

____

____

____

____

____

____

____

____

____

____

____

____

____

____

CHAPTER 4

BUILDING LEADERS WHILE YOU LEAD

Leadership is less about being in charge and more about being who you needed when you were starting out.

Finally, Oakland Gardens was stabilizing. We'd gone from chaos to consistency, from $300,000 to seven-figure production. The team was working together. Patients were coming back. For the first time in years, the practice felt alive.

But stabilization is just the beginning. Now came the harder part: developing people while managing the daily operations, handling crises that could destroy everything, and somehow not losing myself in the process.

Mary's voice never left me. Even though I was on my own now, her leadership style lived rent-free in my head. When I was unsure, I asked myself, "What would Mary do?" When the team pushed back, I thought, "How would Mary handle this?" And when I saw someone struggling, I leaned in—just like she did with me.

STEPPING INTO THE ROLE OF MENTOR

The assistants at Oakland Gardens were mostly trained—but poorly. They had the basics down, but there was a lot of unlearning that needed to happen. Sloppy habits, cutting corners, missing details that mattered.

> ### 🎨 *Manager Musings*
>
> *"People don't fail because they're incapable. They fail because no one took the time to show them they could succeed."*

One assistant in particular caught my attention. She had potential but zero confidence. She'd been berated by the previous manager so often that she flinched when anyone approached her. She second-guessed everything, apologized constantly, and was about one bad day from quitting.

I saw myself in her—that hunger mixed with fear, that desire to do well but not knowing how. So, I started investing, like Mary did with me. Not with formal training sessions or big announcements. Just small, consistent deposits of knowledge and confidence.

Within six months, she'd transformed. And that transformation—watching someone go from barely surviving to genuinely thriving—that's what mentorship is really about. It's not about creating carbon copies of yourself. It's about helping people discover their own strengths and giving them permission to use them.

THE FOUR LEVELS OF LEADERSHIP DEVELOPMENT

Through developing my team members at Oakland Gardens, I discovered there are four distinct levels of growth:

Level 1: The Demonstration Phase

Show them exactly how it's done. Not just the task, but the standard. The attention to detail. The pride in the work. They watch, you do.

Level 2: The Collaboration Phase

Work alongside them. You do it together. They handle the parts they're comfortable with, you fill in the gaps. Real-time correction without criticism.

Level 3: The Supervised Independence Phase

They do, you observe. Bite your tongue when they do it differently than you would. Let them find their own rhythm as long as the outcome meets the standard.

Level 4: The Teaching Phase

They know it well enough to teach someone else. This is when you know the mentorship has taken root—when they can pass it forward.

STILL MAKING MISTAKES—STILL LEARNING

I was getting better, but I wasn't perfect. Not even close.

One day, I hired someone without checking references because they interviewed well and we desperately needed help. They lasted two weeks before disappearing with a day's worth of copayments. Desperation makes you stupid. Always check references.

The result was chaos—double-bookings, gaps, frustrated patients, and a near-revolt from the team. I learned the hard way: change without preparation is just chaos with extra steps.

I started keeping a notebook, documenting every mistake that cost time, money, or trust. That notebook became my most valuable training tool, both for myself and for developing others.

BECOMING THE CALM IN THE CHAOS

As Oakland Gardens improved, I noticed something: The better things got, the more the team looked to me for emotional stability. When a patient screamed at the front desk, they looked to see how I'd react. When insurance claims got denied in bulk, they watched my response. When equipment failed, schedules imploded, or staff called out sick, all eyes turned to me.

I learned that a leader's emotional state is contagious. If I panicked, everyone panicked. If I stayed calm, the team found their footing.

This didn't mean hiding stress or pretending everything was fine. It meant:

- Taking a breath before responding to any crisis
- Asking "What do we need to solve first?" instead of "Why did this happen?"

- Maintaining perspective: "Will this matter in a week? A month? A year?"
- Showing confidence in the team's ability to handle challenges

But maintaining this calm was exhausting. Every night I went home carrying the weight of being everyone's anchor. The stress was building, even as our success grew.

There were always hiccups and fires that needed putting out, like when I lost one of my top-performing front desk team members. She was my right hand—dependable, sharp, quick with patients, and totally in sync with me. The day she left, I felt gutted. Not just because I liked her, but because I knew what came next. I'd have to find someone new. Start the hiring process. Hope they'd show up on time. Hope they'd catch on fast. And in the meantime? I'd be doing her job, my job, and the job of training the next person—maybe even for weeks.

I felt alone. Overwhelmed. Frustrated. And then it hit me— that's probably exactly how Mary felt when I left.

I sat with that realization for a while. But I didn't have long to dwell on it.

DRAWING THE LINE—EVEN WHEN IT'S UNCOMFORTABLE

One day, I found a small bag tucked in a corner of the office— behind a cabinet where one assistant often took breaks. Inside was a small amount of white powder—and I didn't need a lab test to know what I was looking at.

My heart dropped. This could destroy everything we'd worked for. The practice's reputation, the team's trust, the progress we'd made. And this particular assistant? She was good at her job, well-liked by patients, part of our success story.

But leadership isn't about easy decisions. As much as it sucked, I had to take action. I decided to first document everything—photos, location, time found. Then I went to the doctors. We agreed we had to involve authorities and terminate the employee, but we'd handle it as quietly and professionally as possible.

The conversation with the assistant was one of the hardest I'd had. She denied it at first, then broke down. She had a problem. She needed help. We gave her resources for treatment, but we couldn't keep her on. The risk to patients, to the practice, and to the other employees was too great.

The team was shaken. Some were angry we'd let her go. Others were relieved. I held a brief meeting. "We've had to make a difficult decision regarding a team member," I told them. "I can't share details, but I want you to know that your safety and our patients' safety will always be my priority. We're moving forward, and we're moving forward together."

That incident taught me that leadership sometimes means making decisions that won't be popular but are necessary. It's not about being liked—it's about protecting what you've all built together.

CRISIS MANAGEMENT PROTOCOL

When facing a serious crisis:

1. **Document everything** before taking action
2. **Consult with ownership/legal** immediately
3. **Act decisively** but with compassion
4. **Communicate what the team needs to know**—not everything, but enough
5. **Support the remaining team** through the transition

THE SUCCESS TRAP

Despite the (many) bumps in the road, Oakland Gardens turned completely around, and the brothers were impressed. More importantly, the team was strong and patients were happy.

The better I got at solving problems, the more problems landed on my desk—not just from Oakland Gardens but from the main office as well. The brothers started having me consult on their other locations. Team members from other practices called me for advice. I was becoming the go-to person for everything.

My days got longer. My phone never stopped. Weekends became planning sessions for the week ahead. I was succeeding professionally but disappearing personally.

If you're one of those people who powers through the day without stopping, let me tell you something: You're a high-performance office manager. You care. You're dialed in. You're the glue holding the office together. But here's the truth I had to learn the hard way—we don't get that time back. And as we get older, those skipped lunches and burned-out days catch up to us. Physically. Mentally. Emotionally.

I still remember standing at the back counter one day, half-eating and half-writing out an insurance narrative by hand. No automated software. No templates. Just me, a pen, and a patient history that needed to be convincing enough to get a claim paid. That was my wake-up call.

I started making a conscious effort to step away. To pause. To breathe. And guess what? Everything kept running. The office survived. The world didn't fall apart because I took twenty minutes to myself.

I didn't realize it until then, but the warning signs had been there all along. Checking emails at my kid's school events. Answering calls during family dinners. Sunday night anxiety

That started Saturday afternoon. I was building something amazing, but I was losing myself in the process.

THE MULTIPLICATION EFFECT

Despite the growing stress, I kept developing people, and every person I developed either multiplied my impact or taught me a lesson. The ones who grew became leaders themselves. The ones who didn't taught me to recognize potential versus wishful thinking.

The more people I developed, the more the brothers noticed. They saw me not just as someone who could manage a practice, but as someone who could build leaders. That visibility would soon lead to an opportunity that looked like a dream but would become my biggest lesson in standing for principles.

The Oakland Gardens turnaround was complete. I'd proven I could take something failing and make it thrive. But that success was about to be tested in ways I never imagined. The brothers had bigger plans for me—plans that would force me to choose between opportunity and integrity, between financial security and personal values.

Next, in Chapter 5, I'll share how a broken promise taught me more than any success could, why divorce and business betrayal happened simultaneously, and how sometimes the worst moments become the catalyst for your greatest transformation.

Who in your life needs you to believe in them before they believe in themselves? What would change if you invested in their potential the way someone once invested in yours?

____

____

____

____

____

____

____

____

____

____

____

____

____

CHAPTER 5

WHEN BROKEN PROMISES FREE YOU

Sometimes life doesn't break you gradually—it shatters you all at once, forcing you to rebuild from pieces you didn't know existed.

The year Oakland Gardens hit seven figures should have been my victory lap. I'd proven I could turn around a failing practice. I'd built a team from scratch. I'd developed systems that worked. The brothers were making more money from that location than they'd ever imagined possible.

But success has a way of revealing character—both yours and others'. And that year, I learned painful truths about promises, partnerships, and the price of trusting the wrong people.

WHEN EVERYTHING FALLS APART AT ONCE

I was going through a divorce—a life quietly unraveling behind the scenes. My marriage had been struggling for years. The long hours, the stress, and the constant focus on work had all taken its toll. We'd grown apart, become roommates rather than partners.

And just as I was trying to hold that part of my life together, the practice I had poured myself into for years was about to be sold out from under me. The two brothers who owned the practice—the ones who had given me my shot, who I'd made wealthy through my work at Oakland Gardens—decided it was time to cash out.

No warning. No discussion. Just a decision that my entire professional world was about to change hands.

A BROKEN PROMISE HURTS MORE THAN A BAD DEAL

The older brother pulled me aside after announcing the sale. He made a promise—said he'd make sure I was taken care of. Called it a "thank-you bonus" for all the work I'd done to grow the practice from the ground up. A reward for turning their disaster into a goldmine.

"Kyle," he said, actually using my name. "You've done something remarkable with Oakland Gardens. We won't forget that."

I believed him. Why wouldn't I? I had basically become that practice. I ran it like an owner. Managed the full staff. Oversaw everything from collections to payroll to treatment plans. I was showing up every day like it was my name on the lease.

When the sale process started, I didn't just step back. I stepped in. I helped show the practice to the potential buyers. Gathered production reports. Pulled collection data. Broke down what we paid the associates. I basically played broker for free—selling a practice I'd built but didn't own.

The sale went through. The brothers got their payout. The bonus they promised me? It never came. Not a penny.

LEADING WHILE BROKEN

During this period of professional betrayal and personal dissolution, I still had to show up every day. Still had to lead the team. Still had to smile at patients. Still had to solve problems.

But I was falling apart inside. The team at Oakland Gardens never knew what I was going through. They saw the same Kyle—maybe a little tired, maybe a little quieter, but still present, still leading, still caring about their development and success.

This is when I learned about compartmentalization—not as denial, but as survival. I developed what I call the "Parking Lot Practice":

THE PARKING LOT PRACTICE:

- Sit in your car before entering work
- Take five deep breaths
- Mentally put your personal problems in a box
- Place that box in the trunk

- Promise yourself you'll pick it up after work
- Walk into work as the leader your team needs

Was it healthy long-term? No. But it got me through the immediate crisis without destroying everything I'd built.

It can be a hard pill to swallow, but sometimes you have to lead while you're broken. Your team doesn't stop needing you because your life is falling apart. Patients don't stop coming because you're getting divorced. Problems don't pause for your personal crises.

The hardest lesson during this time was understanding that my pain wasn't something I could bring through those office doors. The team had their own struggles—sick kids, aging parents, and their own relationship problems. They needed a leader, not another burden. So I learned to carry it alone, at least during business hours.

I also discovered that consistency mattered more than perfection. There were days I could barely function at seventy percent capacity, but I showed up anyway. And you know what? Seventy percent of a leader is better than an empty office. The team needed to see me there, even if I wasn't at my best. They needed the stability of knowing someone was at the helm, even if that someone was quietly drowning.

Work became a strange kind of refuge during this period. When everything at home felt like it was dissolving—lawyers, paperwork, dividing assets, custody schedules—the office problems felt manageable. A scheduling conflict? I could fix that. An insurance denial? There was an appeal process. A difficult patient? I knew how to handle it. These were solvable problems, unlike the mess waiting for me at home.

But I had to learn the hard way that while work could be a temporary escape, it wasn't therapy. I still needed actual support, actual help, actual healing—things a dental office couldn't provide, no matter how many problems I solved there.

THE FIVE STAGES OF DENTAL MANAGEMENT BURNOUT

Burnout doesn't happen overnight. It's a slow burn that takes years to fully ignite, and by the time you smell smoke, you're already on fire. For dental office managers, it follows a predictable pattern—especially when you're dealing with practice drama, ownership changes, or personal crises alongside professional demands.

Step 1: The Honeymoon Phase:

Everything feels like growth. You're building something important. Twelve-hour days feel like investments in your future. You're needed, valued, essential. The adrenaline of solving problems masks the exhaustion. You tell yourself the pace is temporary.

Step 2: The Onset of Stress:

The excitement fades but the workload doesn't. Lunch becomes optional. Weekends become catch-up time. You check emails at your kid's soccer game. But you push through because you're "almost there"—wherever "there" is.

Step 3: Chronic Stress:

Always behind, never caught up. Your family stops expecting you at dinner. Your back hurts constantly. You've gained weight or lost too much. But success is just around the corner, right? This is what dedication looks like... right?

Step 4: Full Burnout:

Your body is at work but your soul has left the building. You resent everything—the patients, the staff, the career you once loved. Physical symptoms multiply: migraines, insomnia, digestive issues. But you can't stop because who else could do this?

Step 5: Habitual Burnout:

This is just who you are now. The office can't function without you, and you've built your entire identity around being indispensable. The thought of boundaries feels like betrayal. You're not living anymore—you're just maintaining. And the scariest part? It feels normal.

STARTING OVER UNDER NEW OWNERSHIP

The dust eventually settled. And when it did, I was still standing. The new owners wanted to keep me on. They recognized what I brought to the table—the systems, the team loyalty, the operational knowledge. But they also made it clear: things would be different under their ownership.

They let go of all the associate dentists except one. Changed insurance plans. Shifted the patient demographic. Everything I'd carefully built was being restructured.

But surprisingly, they gave me more autonomy than the brothers ever had. They valued my input. They listened to my concerns. They treated me less like an employee and more like a partner—the very thing the brothers had promised but never delivered.

The new owners weren't perfect, but they were fair. They honored their word. They paid on time. They gave me room to grow. After what I'd been through with the brothers, basic professional decency felt revolutionary.

THE WISDOM IN THE WOUNDS

That year taught me things success never could.

The first lesson: promises without paper are just conversation. When the brothers' bonus never materialized, I learned to stop banking on words. Now, if it matters, it goes in writing. Not because I don't trust people, but because even well-meaning people can have selective memories when money's involved.

The broken promise also taught me something about my own worth. For weeks after the sale, I questioned everything. Was I not valuable enough? Had I not done enough? But eventually I realized their inability to keep their word said nothing about my value and everything about their character. I'd taken their practice from barely surviving to seven figures. That achievement didn't disappear just because they couldn't acknowledge it with a check.

The strangest part? Once I understood all this, I stopped being angry. The best revenge wasn't rage or retaliation—it was the success that came after. Not to prove something to them, but to prove to myself what I was capable of when I stopped waiting for permission to be valuable.

They did me a favor, really. They forced me to see that I'd been undervaluing myself long before they broke their promise.

Next, in Chapter 6, I'll share how I navigated insurance chaos, firing a dentist, and ended up in court as a witness, and how the worst job of my career taught me the most valuable lessons about standing for what's right.

What promise has been broken in your life that might actually be freeing you for something better? What would you do if you stopped waiting for someone else's permission to value yourself appropriately?

CHAPTER 6

OVERCOMING INSURANCE CHAOS AND COURT CASES

Leadership isn't just about helping patients say yes, but knowing what you're saying yes to behind the scenes.

With the two new owners came a whole new world of dentistry I thought I understood—until I didn't. Suddenly, we were credentialed with just about every dental insurance plan known to man. PPOs, DMOs, HMOs, Medicaid, union plans—the whole alphabet soup. The office that once ran on straightforward co-pays and basic benefits turned into an insurance minefield overnight.

A CRASH COURSE IN INSURANCE CHAOS

Some plans paid seventy-five cents for an X-ray. The film alone costs more than that. The electricity to run the machine costs more. Hell, the patient probably paid more to park their car outside.

Then there were the dreaded DHMO plans—the ones where practices get a small monthly capitation fee whether the patient shows up or not. You're basically incentivized not to treat patients. The more work you do, the more money you lose. It's healthcare turned completely upside down.

And with that shift in insurance came a shift in patients. We went from working-class families with traditional PPO coverage to a completely different patient base. More Medicaid. More union plans. More people were coming in confused about what their plan even covered—if anything.

And guess who had to explain it all? Me. I became the insurance expert, whether I wanted to or not.

I started learning the patterns. Which plans always denied certain procedures, which plans required pre-authorization for everything, and which would automatically downgrade codes no matter how well you documented. I created spreadsheets, tracked reimbursements, and identified which procedure-plan combinations actually lost us money.

Within months, I could predict what any insurance plan would pay for any procedure. I knew which narratives would get approved, which wouldn't. I knew which plans to fight and which weren't worth the effort.

> ⚙ **Manager Musings**
>
> *"Insurance doesn't care about your patient. But you do. And that's why you have to become the translator between the two."*

CASE ACCEPTANCE IN A NEW WORLD

Every day brought new denials, new downgrades, and new ways insurance companies found to not pay for legitimate treatment. But this experience became invaluable. Because once you understand how insurance companies think—how they're designed to deny first and ask questions later—you can start working the system instead of being worked by it.

This new insurance landscape changed everything I thought I knew about case acceptance. Before, it was about walking a patient through the value of treatment, discussing out-of-pocket costs, and helping them feel comfortable with saying yes. Now? It was about managing expectations when insurance paid little to nothing, and patients assumed everything was covered.

It tested my communication skills, my patience, and my ability to deliver bad news without losing trust. There were times I'd present a treatment plan and a patient would say, "Wait... my insurance doesn't cover this?" And I'd have to say, "Not even close."

Day after day, I'd watch faces fall and witness trust eroding—not in us, but in the system they'd been paying into for years. I had to find ways to talk about value over cost. Long-term health over short-term savings. It wasn't easy, but it made me sharper, more empathetic, and more honest.

THE INSURANCE REALITY CONVERSATION

Every dental office manager becomes a professional dream-crusher the moment they explain what insurance actually covers. You watch hope die in patients' eyes when they realize their "comprehensive coverage" barely covers a cleaning. But this conversation doesn't have to destroy trust—it can build it, if you handle it right.

Start with the reset:

Before diving into treatment, reset their insurance expectations completely. "Your insurance works differently than you probably think. They pay a percentage of what they think a procedure should cost, not what it actually costs. They think a crown should cost $500. It actually costs $1,200." Use real numbers from their plan, not generic examples.

Pivot to health:

Once they understand the insurance limitations, shift focus. "Now let's forget about insurance for a moment and talk about what's actually happening in your mouth." Show them X-rays. Explain the consequences of waiting. Make it about health, not coverage.

Always provide three options:

The ideal treatment plan (everything done right), the phased approach (spreading cost over time), and the bare minimum (addressing only urgent issues). Let them choose their path based on their situation, not your assumption.

Document everything:

Not just what treatment was presented, but what the patient understood about costs, what option they chose, and why. This protects everyone, even when, six months later, they've forgotten the conversation and wonder why insurance didn't cover their crown.

I developed strategies for every type of disappointment. For the patient who thought everything was covered. For the one who couldn't afford the necessary treatment. For the one who felt betrayed by the insurance they'd paid into for years.

Some days I felt more like a grief counselor than an office manager, helping people process the loss of what they thought they had—comprehensive coverage—and accept the reality of what they actually had.

FROM MANAGING INSURANCE TO FIRING A DENTIST

As I mentioned earlier, the two new owners made a bold decision to let go of all the associate dentists except one. The one they kept? Let's just say it was complicated.

Tension had been building between him and the new owners for a while. It started with quiet friction, turned into closed-door disagreements, and eventually escalated into outright conflict. The atmosphere in the office became toxic. You could feel it in the hallways. Patients could sense it. Staff started taking sides.

One day, while the new owners were working from their other office, I received an email. Attached to it was a letter. "Give this to him," the email read. "It's his termination notice."

I stared at the screen. My stomach sank. They weren't even in the building. They were miles away at their other location, safe from the confrontation they were forcing me into.

So there I was, tasked with holding a printed letter in front of a man who had been practicing dentistry longer than I had been alive, about to tell him he no longer worked here. The walk to his office felt like a death march. My mouth was dry. My heart was pounding so hard I was sure he could hear it.

"I need to speak with you privately," I managed to say.

He looked up from his charts, saw my face, and knew. You could see it in his eyes—first confusion, then realization, then anger.

"The owners have instructed me to give you this."

He stared at me. Silent at first. Reading. Processing. And then it came—the explosion. The anger, the disbelief, the accusations, the threats of legal action. He called the owners cowards, and honestly, I couldn't disagree. But I had to stand there, professional and calm, absorbing his rage while wanting to scream that this wasn't my choice.

And then I had to do something I'll never forget:

"Before you leave... I need the office key."

That moment felt like it lasted an hour. Asking a professional, a doctor, someone with decades of experience, to hand over his key like he was some kind of criminal. My hands trembled as I held them out.

The key hit my palm harder than it needed to. He gathered his things in hostile silence, and I had to escort him to the doors. Past the staff who were pretending not to watch. Past patients in the waiting room. Past everything he'd helped build.

I wasn't just delivering bad news—I was the face of his professional execution. And in that moment, I felt the full weight of being "the manager."

> ### 🧠 *Manager Musings*
>
> *"Leadership isn't always meetings and metrics. Sometimes, it's courtrooms, conflict, and survival."*

FROM DENTAL OFFICE MANAGER TO WITNESS IN COURT

It didn't end there. Shortly after, I found myself dragged into a legal battle. The dentist didn't go quietly. He sued. I was now caught in a legal storm of deposition dates, subpoenas, and courtroom obligations for a battle I didn't even start.

They grilled me on the 'intent' behind someone else's decisions—decisions I was only following, not making:

"What did you understand about the reasons for termination?"

"Did you witness any conversations about treatment planning?"

"Were you aware of any billing practices that concerned you?"

I answered every question the best I could. Carefully. Truthfully. Professionally. But inside, I was screaming: "I'm just the office manager!"

WHEN YOU'RE CAUGHT IN LEGAL CROSSFIRE

Being subpoenaed or deposed in someone else's lawsuit is terrifying. You didn't create the conflict, but suddenly you're in the middle of it, being questioned about decisions you didn't make and conversations you barely remember. Whether it's a wrongful termination suit, an insurance fraud investigation, or a partnership dispute, your role as office manager makes you a key witness to everything.

The Golden Rule:

Tell the truth, even when it's uncomfortable. But only the truth you actually know. "I don't know" and "I don't remember" are complete, acceptable answers. Never speculate about what someone meant or intended—you're not a mind reader. Answer only what's asked, nothing more. That helpful instinct to over-explain? Kill it. Extra words become extra problems in legal proceedings.

The Protection Protocol:

Get your own lawyer—not the practice's lawyer. Before any deposition, document everything you remember while it's fresh. Keep copies of concerning documents stored outside the office (they can't subpoena what they don't know exists). Understand your state's whistleblower protections in case you need them.

The Reality Check:

You're not on trial, but it'll feel like you are. Every word will be scrutinized. Your loyalty will be tested. You'll leave exhausted and second-guessing everything you said. But remember: your only obligation is to the truth, not to either party. You didn't create this mess, and it's not your job to clean it up—just to honestly report what you saw.

In short, the dentist claimed the new owners were committing insurance fraud. He accused them of manipulating treatment plans, upcoding procedures, skipping over conservative care, going straight from a simple filling to a root canal when intermediate steps might have saved the tooth, skipping composite fillings and pushing crowns that were rushed and sloppy, and so on.

While those accusations were pointed at the owners, I felt them hitting me. I was the one submitting the claims after all. I was the one helping build the treatment plans. I was the one the patients saw. The one they trusted when they asked, "Is this really necessary?"

GROWING SEEDS OF DOUBT

I felt exposed. Embarrassed. And, truthfully, a little betrayed. Not necessarily because the accusations were true, but because they made me question everything. Every treatment plan I'd presented. Every claim I'd submitted. Every time I'd assured a patient that yes, this treatment was necessary.

I wondered whether the decisions I had supported and the plans I had presented were all above board. It shook my confidence. It planted doubts I couldn't ignore.

By this point in my career, I had so much dental IQ from years of observing treatment planning. I could often spot when something was truly necessary or when it felt like overkill. When a conservative approach might work, but wasn't even discussed. When we jumped straight to the most expensive option.

I told myself I wasn't the dentist. I didn't have the license. It wasn't my call. But deep down, I was questioning everything—feeling the burden of recommendations I didn't believe in but still delivered. Every aggressive treatment plan I presented felt like a betrayal of patient trust.

That guilt was heavier than the court case itself. Because while I could answer their legal questions about procedures and policies, I couldn't answer the question that kept me up at night: Was I complicit in something wrong?

> ### 🧠 *Manager Musings*
>
> *"You don't have to be the one making the decision to feel the weight of it. Sometimes, just being the messenger is enough to carry the guilt."*

The lawsuit dragged on for months. More depositions. More questions. More doubt. The legal proceedings eventually settled, as these things do. But the damage was done. Not legal damage—a moral injury. The kind that makes you look at yourself in the mirror and wonder who you've become. The kind that makes you realize that "just following orders" is what everyone says right before they admit they knew better. Sometimes you need a lawsuit to make you question your role in a system you've been perpetuating.

Next, in Chapter 7, I'll share how the weight of everything—the court case, the ethical doubts, and years of relentless grinding—finally caught up with me. You'll learn why I walked into a community college and started taking science classes, what happened when I asked for a five-dollar raise and was told I already made "too much," and how getting fired became the best thing that ever happened to my career.

What situation in your current role is testing your integrity? What would need to change for you to feel proud of every treatment plan you present? Sometimes recognizing the misalignment is the first step toward finding your way back to your values.

____

____

____

____

____

____

____

____

____

____

____

____

____

____

CHAPTER 7

GETTING FIRED INTO YOUR FUTURE

Sometimes it's not the burnout that breaks you—it's the moment you realize you've been surviving instead of living.

After the court appearances, the accusations, the deposition, and the emotional weight of a divorce that was grinding through my personal life like a slow-moving disaster, I started to unravel slowly.

Don't get me wrong—I was still doing the job, still leading the team, and still making things happen. But I was just running on autopilot and going through the motions with a smile on my face while something inside me had started to crack.

THE BURNOUT I COULDN'T IGNORE ANYMORE

For years, I had taken pride in my ability to handle pressure. I thrived in chaos. Lived for the challenges. I'd outwork, outthink, and outlast anyone. But now? I was tired—physically, emotionally, ethically, and even existentially. I didn't know if I wanted to keep doing this.

For the first time in my career, I no longer felt aligned with the work. The accusations from the lawsuit haunted me, forcing me to look at patterns I'd been ignoring: Treatment plans that seemed aggressive, procedures that jumped to expensive options, and—worst of all—my role in presenting these plans to trusting patients.

> 🧠 ***Manager Musings***
>
> *"Being good at case acceptance doesn't mean saying yes to every case. It means having the guts to ask: is this truly what's best for the patient?"*

Through the years, with Mary's mentorship and from managing for so long, I had learned something important about myself: I was really good at getting patients to say yes. Not just good—exceptional. I knew how to connect. I knew how to build.

trust. I knew how to guide people toward decisions that would change their health and their lives.

I wasn't just presenting treatment plans. I was driving the practice's future every time I helped a patient move forward. So, why was I still the middleman? Why was I still pouring myself into someone else's vision?

That's when the idea started to creep in. "Maybe I'm supposed to be the one in the operatory," I wondered. "Maybe I should be the one diagnosing, not just translating someone else's diagnosis." The thought began to take shape: "What if I became a dentist? What if I opened my own practice—built around the very skills that had brought me this far—and hired dentists to work for me?"

It sounded crazy at first. I had a reputation. I was well-connected. I was comfortable. Why would I risk all that? But once the thought entered my mind, it didn't leave. In fact, it only got louder.

COMMUNITY COLLEGE AND A NEW DREAM

The following year, I walked into a local community college and started asking about science classes. Pre-reqs. Pathways into dentistry. I didn't know where it would lead. I didn't even know if I had what it took, but I knew I couldn't keep going the way I was going.

I signed up for classes. I told no one, not even my coworkers. I'd attend evening lectures after work, sometimes exhausted, sometimes energized—but always committed. Biology at 6 PM. Chemistry at 7:30 PM. Home by 10 PM to do homework until midnight. Up at 6 AM to do it all over again.

I didn't expect to become a dentist overnight. I was reclaiming agency more than anything. For so long, I had been a voice between patients and doctors. Now, I wanted to be the one who actually knew—not just professionally, but clinically. Because deep down, I knew I had more to give.

I'd work all day, go straight to class, then come home and try to cram in study time or squeeze in assignments between insurance narratives and weekly reports. There were days I wondered what I was doing to myself. I wasn't a kid anymore. I had real bills, real responsibilities, and barely any sleep. But I stuck it out. I kept telling myself, "This isn't forever. This is for a better version of me."

THE EDUCATION-WHILE-WORKING SURVIVAL GUIDE

Working full-time in dental and going back to school can be a circus of juggling both your schedule and sanity. Whether you're a dental assistant taking business courses, a hygienist pursuing management certification, or a front desk studying practice administration, the challenge is the same: becoming more while maintaining everything you already are.

The Reality:

You'll work all day, attend class all evening, study all night, and somehow still show up smiling for tomorrow's morning huddle. Your coworkers won't understand why you're doing this to yourself. Your family will see you less often. Your body will run on caffeine and determination.

The Strategy:

Take it one semester at a time. Don't calculate how many are left—that math will break you. Celebrate passing grades, not perfect ones. Find at least one person who gets why you're doing this (e.g., your spouse, best friend, coach, etc.), because on the nights when you're studying insurance codes instead of sleeping, you'll need someone to remind you this is temporary.

The Payoff:

Yes, the degree itself opens doors—it's the difference between "years of experience" and "qualified candidate" on job postings. But beyond the credentials, every class you pass is immediately applicable at work. You'll understand the "why" behind policies you used to just follow. You'll speak up in meetings with newfound confidence. And when that promotion finally comes—because it will—you'll have both the paper and the knowledge to back it up.

A FAMILIAR FORK IN THE ROAD

Eventually, a periodontist joined our office. He was sharp, focused, and easy to work with. He brought not just a specialty, but a new level of energy and production that took our numbers to another level. His cases boosted collections. His demeanor boosted morale.

Patients loved him. Staff loved him. And honestly? So did I. Working with him felt different. He was like a machine—and so was I. He would see forty, sometimes fifty patients a day, while I cranked out treatment plans and case presentations nonstop. It was fast-paced. It was exhilarating. And for a while, it was fun again.

Better yet, he added real value to the practice, which helped me hit my monthly bonus goals. Every case accepted meant more money in my pocket—and I was grinding to make it happen. It felt like growth. It felt like progress.

But deep down, something wasn't right. While I was growing my income, I was also strengthening the golden handcuffs. The entrepreneurial fire I once had was quietly dying out, smothered by comfort and paychecks.

Meanwhile, behind the scenes, my college struggles told a different story. After about four years of night school and grinding away, the truth became undeniable: My grades weren't good enough for dental school. Classes like organic chemistry and advanced math were way out of my league. Science wasn't my strength, and dental schools focused almost entirely on science GPA.

There was no possible path forward. No backup plan. No second chance. It crushed me at first. I had poured so much time, money, and energy into the idea of becoming a dentist—of flipping the script and building something of my own. But that door had slammed shut. So, I kept doing what I knew best: managing.

KNOWING YOUR WORTH

With the dental school dream dead, I needed to recalibrate. If I was going to stay in management, I at least wanted to be compensated fairly. So I asked the owners for a raise: five dollars an hour. It could've been my way of trying to feel better about the door that had just closed with school. A small win, to make up for a significant loss.

I walked into the office, sat down across from them, and said it plainly: "I'd like a $5 raise."

Their response? "You already make too much for a dental office manager."

That line broke my heart. Not just because of the money, but because it confirmed something I had been trying to ignore: They didn't value me. They never really had.

I helped build their practice. I poured my heart and soul into it. And to them, I was still just "the manager." Disposable. Replaceable. It was like a kick to the face.

Dejected, I started looking for a new opportunity. I hit Craigslist—which, at the time, was the go-to place for job hunting—and started lining up interviews across New York City. I'd leave the office in the middle of the day sometimes, racing through traffic, chasing the hope of something better.

The sneaking around was obvious. The mysterious "appointments." The vague explanations about where I'd been. The interview clothes barely hidden in my car. And while I was out desperately trying to escape, someone was paying attention.

The periodontist pulled me aside one afternoon. "You've been interviewing," he said. Not a question. A statement.

I froze. Was he going to report me to the owners? Was this about to get worse?

"I'm thinking about purchasing a practice that's in trouble," he continued. "I could use someone who knows how to turn things around. Why don't you come work with me?"

This was someone who'd watched me work, who'd seen what I could do with case acceptance, with operations, with building systems from chaos. He wasn't offering me a position—he was offering me a chance to do what I did best, but with someone who actually valued it. I had the skills. I had the experience. I knew exactly what it took to resurrect a dying practice because I'd already done it. Now someone was finally willing to bet on me.

"Yes," I said, without hesitation. "Absolutely."

For the first time in a long time, I felt that entrepreneurial spark flicker back to life. Maybe my path wasn't dead. Maybe it just needed a different door.

> ### 🧠 *Manager Musings*
>
> *"Sometimes the door doesn't open until you're brave enough to ask for more—and willing to walk if you don't get it."*

THE MESSY TRANSITION

His new practice was a disaster, but it was now my disaster. A chance to build something right. To create systems that worked. To develop a team that thrived. To serve patients without compromising integrity.

At first, I split my time between the old office and the new one. But it didn't take long for the owners to get annoyed. They didn't like me taking days off—even though I was salaried. The truth is, salary isn't always a blessing. Sometimes, it's a leash. You're expected to show up no matter what, for a flat rate, even when your heart and effort have moved on.

Before long, the owners pulled me into a meeting. They told me they would be cutting my salary, docking $200 for every day I missed. It scared me. Because honestly, he couldn't afford to pay me enough yet to cover that loss. But I knew one thing for sure: I wasn't going backward.

I smiled, nodded, and said, "I understand."

They cut my pay. I took the hit. And I figured it out. For a few months, I juggled the chaos—piecing things together, surviving the gap. Until one day, I got the call: "Kyle, the doctors have asked you not to return to the office."

Fired. Just like that.

I was relieved. This wasn't the end. This was the beginning.

SAME TEST, DIFFERENT TEACHER

The irony wasn't lost on me. Another disaster. Another team that needed rebuilding. Another complete transformation. I'd done this before—and watched other people profit from it.

Not this time.

> 🧠 *Manager Musings*
>
> *"The universe has a sense of humor. It keeps giving you the same test until you finally take it for yourself instead of making someone else rich."*

The periodontist had watched me work. He knew what I could do. He'd offered me this opportunity because he respected my abilities—not as overhead to be minimized, but as a partner in success. Oakland Gardens had been my masterclass in transformation. Now I'd finally get to use that education for myself.

Next, in Chapter 8, I'll share how walking into that failing practice felt like déjà vu, why building from the bottom again taught me more than any degree could, and how creating culture became more important than creating systems.

Think about a skill you've perfected while building someone else's dream. What would change if you finally used that expertise for your own growth instead of theirs? Sometimes the best revenge against being undervalued isn't walking away—it's succeeding so visibly that they can't ignore what they lost.

CHAPTER 8

BUILDING FROM THE BOTTOM (AGAIN)

Sometimes the best opportunities look like abandoned buildings—you just need the vision to see the blueprint hidden in the ruins.

There's a strange kind of peace that comes after you've lost what you thought you needed most. No more pretending. No more fighting for scraps. I was finally free—and it was time to build something better.

The periodontist's new office wasn't glamorous. The phones barely rang. The schedule had more holes than Swiss cheese. Every month, the overhead numbers made it look like we were fighting a losing battle. But where others saw a sinking ship, I saw a blank canvas. This time, I wasn't following someone else's playbook. I was writing my own.

DÉJÀ VU

Walking into that practice felt eerily familiar. The same untapped potential buried under dysfunction. The same resigned faces. The same systems held together with duct tape and desperation.

But this time, I had something I didn't have before: proof. I'd already turned one disaster into a success. And I'd learned the hard way that real turnarounds don't start with better systems— they start with better culture.

The first thing I did wasn't pull the reports. It wasn't audit the schedule. It wasn't check the insurance backlog. It was to listen and observe.

I sat with the existing staff—and asked the simplest questions:

- "What's working here?"
- "What's not?"
- "What would make this place better?"

Most of them had never been asked those questions before. And that's when I realized how broken things really were—not just operationally, but emotionally.

The periodontist they had worked for all those years had retired unexpectedly due to illness. Their world had changed overnight. And now here we were—the new owner and myself, fresh off the chaos of my last job—ready to rebuild.

But I knew something they didn't know about me: I had been through this before. I had lived the uneasy feeling of a practice changing hands. I knew what it felt like to wonder if the new leadership would respect what you had built—or erase it. Even if they didn't show it on their faces, I knew exactly what they were feeling.

And because of that, I approached this transition carefully and strategically—but above all, emotionally.

THE INHERITED TEAM ASSESSMENT MATRIX

Some of the staff were ready to build. You could feel their energy. They wanted to turn the page. But others? They were already halfway out the door—emotionally checked out, quietly planning their exit.

When you inherit a team, you inherit their history. Not everyone will be willing—or able—to build something new. And that's okay. You can't force people to stay on a journey they're no longer committed to. You can only lead the ones who are ready to move forward.

When you take over an existing team, not everyone is in the same place emotionally or professionally. Understanding where each person stands helps you lead appropriately.

THE ENERGIZERS (READY TO BUILD)

- **Signs**: Ask questions about the future, volunteer for new projects, show up early to changes
- **Your approach**: Give them ownership, involve them in planning, make them ambassadors
- **Timeline**: Engage immediately—they're your momentum builders

THE WAIT-AND-SEE (CAUTIOUSLY HOPEFUL)

- **Signs**: Polite but reserved, follow instructions but don't volunteer, watch more than participate
- **Your approach**: Consistent communication, small wins to build trust, patient inclusion
- **Timeline**: Usually decide within 60–90 days

THE GRIEVERS (PROCESSING LOSS)

- **Signs**: Talk often about "how things used to be," compare everything to the past, emotional about changes
- **Your approach**: Acknowledge what was good before, honor the legacy while building forward, give space
- **Timeline**: May need 3–6 months to fully transition (or may never)

THE EXITS (ALREADY GONE)

- **Signs**: Minimum effort, resistant to all change, negative influence on others, frequent absences
- **Your approach**: Direct conversation about expectations, clear timeline for improvement, document everything
- **Timeline**: Usually self-select out within 60 days if culture changes

The truth is, you can't save everyone. Focus your energy on the Energizers and Wait-and-See groups. The Exits will either rise to the new standard or remove themselves.

THE LIKABLE LEADER WHO COULDN'T LEAD

There was already an office manager in place when I arrived. He wasn't a bad person—far from it. He was well-liked by staff and patients alike. He smiled a lot. He had a nickname for every patient. He kept the energy light. But leadership? It wasn't there.

> **⚙ Manager Musings**
>
> *"Being liked isn't the same as being effective. Some of the nicest people in your office might be the ones holding it back—not because they're bad, but because they've confused warmth with leadership."*

Billing was messy. Collections were inconsistent. Scheduling had no real system. The cracks weren't personal—they were operational. I tried to coach him. Patiently. I showed him cleaner processes. I encouraged him to take ownership. I gave him opportunities to lead. But deep down, he didn't want to change. He was comfortable. And comfort, I realized, is the biggest enemy of progress.

Eventually, he chose to leave on his own. There was no drama. No confrontation. Just a quiet ending to an era that needed to end. And just like that—I was now fully at the helm of the day-to-day operations.

THE COMFORT VS. GROWTH DIAGNOSTIC

How do you know if someone on your team is too comfortable to grow? Look for these patterns:

Signs of Productive Comfort:

- Confident in their role but still learning
- Efficient because they've mastered basics, not because they've stopped trying
- Comfortable enough to take risks and suggest improvements
- Uses stability as a platform for innovation

Signs of Dangerous Comfort:

- Resistant to any change, even obviously beneficial ones
- "We've always done it this way" as a default response
- Avoids new responsibilities or learning opportunities
- Defensive when given feedback
- Others work around them rather than through them

The Coaching Conversation: If you identify someone in dangerous comfort, have a direct conversation:

1. "I've noticed [specific behavior]. Help me understand your perspective."
2. "What would need to change for you to feel excited about growth here?"
3. "Here's what I need from someone in your role going forward..."
4. "What support would help you get there?"

Give them 30–60 days with clear milestones. Document everything. Most will either rise to the challenge or decide to leave on their own—which is often the healthiest outcome for everyone.

WHEN ACCOUNTABILITY MEETS KINDNESS

The transition wasn't easy for anyone. At first, the team was hesitant. But slowly, they saw I wasn't there to tear down what they loved. I was there to build something they could love again. Something sustainable. Something worth staying for.

And that shift? It didn't happen because I demanded it. It happened because I stayed consistent, clear, and compassionate through every step.

We started laying the foundation for something different:

- We created a mission—not a corporate slogan, but words we actually believed.

- We defined our expectations—specific, measurable, non-negotiable.

- We brought accountability—with kindness.

- And we celebrated every small win like it was the Super Bowl.

BUILDING CULTURE FROM SCRATCH

Culture isn't a poster on the wall. It's the answer to the question: "How do we actually treat each other around here?" Here's how to build it intentionally:

STEP 1: DEFINE YOUR NON-NEGOTIABLES (WEEK 1–2)

Pick three to five behaviors that define your culture. Not aspirations—actual standards. Examples:

- "We don't talk about patients negatively, ever"

- "Problems get raised immediately, not saved for later"

- "We answer phones by the second ring" Make them specific enough to observe and measure.

STEP 2: MODEL FIRST, MANDATE SECOND (WEEK 2–4)

Before expecting behavior from others, demonstrate it yourself—consistently, visibly, repeatedly. Your team is watching to see if you're serious or if this is just another initiative that'll fade.

STEP 3: CELEBRATE PUBLICLY, CORRECT PRIVATELY (ONGOING)

When someone embodies your culture, call it out in front of everyone. When someone violates it, address it immediately but behind closed doors. The ratio should be 5:1 positive to corrective.

STEP 4: CONNECT CULTURE TO RESULTS (MONTHLY)

Show the team how culture drives outcomes. "Our patient satisfaction went up because we've been doing X." "Collections improved because we committed to Y." Make the connection explicit.

STEP 5: HIRE AND FIRE BY CULTURE (ONGOING)

Every hiring decision should include culture fit. Every termination conversation should reference culture violations. When your team sees you protect the culture, they'll protect it too.

TURNING CULTURE INTO COLLECTIONS

Culture doesn't only revolve around making people feel good. When you build a strong culture, you're also creating an environment where people want to show up, want to contribute, and take pride in their work.

And when that happens? The numbers move. The phones ring. The schedule fills. The energy shifts—and so does the bottom line.

Little by little, the same office that once felt stuck in survival mode began to thrive. Patients could feel it. Staff could feel it. And the collections could prove it.

It didn't happen overnight. It happened because we stayed consistent. We stuck to our mission. We communicated clearly. We celebrated wins, corrected misses, and showed up for each other every single day.

For the first time, I wasn't just managing a practice. I was creating a machine—a culture-driven, case-accepting, referral-generating, high-energy machine. And every success we had—every patient who said "yes," every month we hit and exceeded our goals—wasn't luck. It was the direct result of the foundation we had fought to build.

Culture had become more than a feeling. It had become a strategy.

THE CULTURE-TO-COLLECTIONS CONNECTION

Skeptics think culture is "soft stuff" that doesn't impact the bottom line. Here's how to prove them wrong:

- Retention Rate: Strong culture = lower turnover. Industry average in dental is 25–30%. Aim for under 15%.

- Case Acceptance: Patients say yes to people they trust. When your team genuinely cares, it shows.

- Referral Rate: Word-of-mouth is free marketing. Strong cultures generate 30–50% referral rates.

When presenting culture initiatives to ownership, don't talk about feelings—talk about these numbers. "Investing in culture isn't about being nice. It translates directly to reducing turn-over costs, increasing case acceptance, and building a referral engine."

YOU CAN'T REINVENT THE WHEEL

Looking back, this turnaround taught me something the first one couldn't: I wasn't lucky. What I'd done before wasn't a fluke—it was a skill. A repeatable process.

But there was a crucial difference this time. I was building with someone who actually valued what I brought to the table. For the first time in my career, I felt like I was working toward something that wasn't going to be taken from me.

The periodontist offered me an opportunity that soon became my proving ground. His practice that had been hemorrhaging staff became the practice people fought to stay at. I learned that culture precedes systems, that not everyone wants to be saved, and that likability isn't leadership.

But most importantly, I proved to both myself and others that I could rebuild the same success no matter the situation. Oakland Gardens wasn't some miracle; it was the beginning of what I was actually capable of.

Next, in Chapter 9, I'll share how scaling the practice meant learning to scale myself—why trying to train someone who didn't want to grow taught me more than any success, and how the seeds of everything I'd later build were planted in frustration.

Think about a team or situation you've inherited. Where does each person fall in the assessment matrix—Energizer, Wait-and-See, Griever, or Exit? What would change if you stopped trying to convert the Exits and invested that energy in your Energizers instead? Sometimes the kindest thing you can do is let people leave who no longer want to be there.

____

____

____

____

____

____

____

____

____

____

____

____

CHAPTER 9

SCALING YOURSELF

The most effective leaders don't wear all the hats—they build a team who can perform even when they're not around.

At this point, I had built something I was proud of. The practice was thriving. The culture was strong. The team trusted the process—and trusted me. But here's the thing no one tells you about leadership: if you don't learn to scale yourself, you eventually become the bottleneck.

I remembered when Mary had given me my first shot at the front desk. The doctor had asked, "Do you think you can ask people for money?" And I had said, "Yes—and I'll do it well." That memory shaped the standard I knew was needed. Not everyone is built to do both: be warm and welcoming while confidently handling money conversations.

THE BOTTLENECK PROBLEM

There's a moment in every leader's career when success becomes its own trap. You've built something amazing. Everyone trusts you. Everyone comes to you. Every decision flows through you.

And then one day you realize: You can't take a vacation. You can't get sick. You can't even step away for a long lunch without your phone buzzing with questions only you can answer. That's when you know you haven't built a system. You've built a dependency.

> ☺ *Manager Musings*
>
> *"Being indispensable feels like job security. It's actually a prison you've built around yourself—one you can't escape until you train someone else to hold the keys."*

I was at that point. The practice was thriving. Everything was running well—as long as I was running it. But what happened when I wasn't there? What happened if I wanted to grow beyond this single location? What happened if I wanted a life outside these walls?

The answer was uncomfortable: everything would fall apart. Because I hadn't built anything that could run without me. I had just stretched myself thinner and thinner.

THE BOTTLENECK SELF-ASSESSMENT

How do you know if you've become the bottleneck? Answer honestly:

Red Flags You're the Bottleneck:

- Your phone buzzes constantly when you're away from the office
- Staff wait for you to make decisions they could make themselves
- You're the only one who knows certain systems or passwords
- Patients specifically ask for you to handle their concerns
- You haven't taken a full day off in months (or years)
- Training new people feels impossible because "it's faster to just do it myself"
- Your team's growth has plateaued because you're not delegating challenging tasks

The Bottleneck Test:

Imagine you had to leave for two weeks with no notice. What would break? Make a list. That list is your roadmap for what needs to be systematized, delegated, or trained.

Scoring:

- 1–2 items: You're in good shape—fine-tune the edges.
- 3–5 items: Warning zone—start delegating immediately.
- 6+ items: Critical—you've built a house of cards with yourself as the foundation.

FINDING THE RIGHT PERSON TO TRAIN

One of the team members had come from the periodontist's father's practice. She was warm, generous, and incredible with patients—remembering every family story, every vacation detail. She had a true heart for people.

But when it came to the financial side—asking for payment, presenting treatment estimates—it wasn't there. No matter how much I coached her, it was always an uphill battle. She hesitated. She avoided. She got too emotionally caught up in wanting to "be nice" instead of confidently advocating for the business.

You can train skills, but you can't teach desire. You can't force someone to learn what they don't want to—or simply can't—absorb. I walked her through why procedures like crown lengthening were needed. I used dental models to explain implants, grafts, and periodontal surgeries. I broke it down in simple terms, hoping it would stick. But most of the time, it didn't.

And eventually, I realized: Some people are great at being welcoming and warm. Others are great at discussing complex treatments and financials. Rarely do you find both in one person. And if you want a truly strong front office—you need both.

That's when I knew: If I wanted the practice to grow, I had to expand the team, not just try to mold one person into something they weren't built for. It was frustrating. It was exhausting at times. But it was one of the biggest leadership lessons I would ever learn.

THE TWO TYPES OF FRONT OFFICE EXCELLENCE

Every successful front office needs a balance of these two skill sets. Understanding the difference will transform how you hire, train, and structure your team.

1) THE RELATIONSHIP BUILDER

Natural Strengths:

- Remembers personal details about patients and their families
- Makes everyone feel welcomed and valued
- Creates emotional connections that build loyalty
- Handles upset patients with empathy and patience
- Generates word-of-mouth referrals through genuine care

Typical Challenges:

- Uncomfortable asking for money
- Avoids difficult financial conversations
- May give away too much (discounts, exceptions) to be "nice"
- Struggles to present large treatment plans confidently
- Takes patient rejections personally

2) THE FINANCIAL CLOSER

Natural Strengths:

- Presents treatment costs without apologizing
- Handles objections professionally and persistently
- Comfortable discussing payment options and financing
- Keeps the business perspective in view
- Closes cases that others might let walk

Typical Challenges:

- May seem too transactional to some patients
- Can miss emotional cues that need addressing first
- Might push too hard before building rapport
- Less patient with "just looking" or indecisive patients
- May not invest in long-term relationship building

THE IDEAL TEAM STRUCTURE:

Don't try to turn one type into the other. Instead, build a team that has both:

- Relationship Builder handles: greeting, scheduling, patient concerns, follow-up calls, recall
- Financial Closer handles: treatment presentations, payment discussions, insurance explanations, collections
- Create a warm handoff between them: "Let me introduce you to Sarah—she'll walk you through everything and answer all your questions about the treatment plan."

THE RARE UNICORN:

Occasionally, you'll find someone who's genuinely strong at both. When you do, pay them well and never let them go. But don't build your system around finding unicorns—build it around leveraging the strengths people actually have.

THE COACHING TRAP

Training someone to grow beyond their natural strengths is harder than just teaching skills. You need patience. You need vision. And you need the wisdom to know when you're pushing harder than they are.

There were so many moments I wanted to step in and say, "Let me just take care of it." And too often, I did. Maybe that was my mistake. Maybe if I had let her struggle more, she would have grown more. Or maybe, no matter how much I coached, she wasn't wired for the deeper clinical and financial understanding that case presentation truly demands.

It taught me a hard truth: You can't want someone's growth more than they do.

THE INVESTMENT DECISION MATRIX

Not every team member deserves the same level of training investment. This isn't about who you like—it's about where your coaching time will generate the best return.

High Potential + High Desire = INVEST HEAVILY

- Signs: Asks questions, practices on their own, takes feedback well, shows improvement
- Your role: Mentor closely, give stretch assignments, prepare them for advancement
- Time investment: 60% of your development energy

High Potential + Low Desire = CHALLENGE

- Signs: Has the skills but coasts, could do more but doesn't, satisfied with "good enough"
- Your role: Direct conversation about expectations, clear consequences, deadline for change
- Time investment: 15% of your development energy (with a deadline)

Low Potential + High Desire = SUPPORT

- Signs: Works hard but hits ceiling, wants to grow but struggles, needs more time for basics
- Your role: Find the right role for their actual abilities, appreciate their effort, be honest about limits
- Time investment: 15% of your development energy

Low Potential + Low Desire = EXIT

- Signs: Minimum effort, resistant to feedback, no improvement over time, negative influence
- Your role: Document, have the conversation, create exit timeline
- Time investment: 10% of your development energy (focused on transition)

The Mistake Most Managers Make: Spending 80% of their energy on the bottom two quadrants—trying to save people who can't or won't be saved—while their high-potential people get neglected and eventually leave.

WHEN "LET ME HANDLE IT" BECOMES THE PROBLEM

I developed a bad habit during this time. Every time a difficult financial conversation came up, every time a treatment presentation got complicated, I'd swoop in.

"Let me just take care of it." It felt efficient. It felt helpful. It felt like I was solving problems. But I was actually creating a bigger one: I was teaching my team that they didn't need to grow because I'd always rescue them.

Looking back, I see the pattern clearly. She'd start a treatment presentation. It would get uncomfortable. She'd look at me with those eyes that said "help." And I'd step in, finish the conversation, close the case. She never had to push through the discomfort. She never had to develop the muscle. Because every time it got hard, I made it easy.

PLANTING SEEDS OF SOMETHING BIGGER

The experience with her was frustrating, but it was also formative. It made me think differently about systems. About training. About how I could create something repeatable—something that didn't rely on one person's "natural" ability or experience.

That's when the early seeds started to form in my mind. A way to break down case presentation into simple, layered steps. A way to help anyone—anyone willing to put in the effort—learn how to guide patients to say yes (more on that later).

For now, the practice kept growing thanks to strong leadership, systems, and culture. But what really fueled the growth was the hard-earned lesson that no matter how good one person is, you grow faster when you build the right team—not just a bigger team.

BUILDING THE *RIGHT* TEAM VS. BUILDING A BIGGER TEAM

There's a critical difference between adding headcount and building capability. Here's how to know which one you need:

Signs You Need the Right Team (Quality Problem):

- Current staff can't handle existing responsibilities well
- You have people in roles that don't match their strengths
- Training the same things repeatedly with no improvement
- One or two people are carrying the rest
- Culture issues that adding people won't solve

Signs You Need a Bigger Team (Capacity Problem):

- Current staff doing excellent work but overwhelmed
- Missing opportunities because no one has bandwidth

- Quality is high but volume is suffering
- Growth is being limited by hours in the day, not skill gaps
- Good people are burning out from overwork

The Sequence That Works:

1. Right people first, then more people
2. Systems first, then scale
3. Culture first, then capacity

The Sequence That Fails:

1. Throwing bodies at problems
2. Hiring before systematizing (just multiplies chaos)
3. Growing before the foundation is solid

The Math:

- 3 wrong people = 0 (or negative) productivity
- 2 right people = 4x productivity (synergy effect)
- 2 right people + systems = 8x productivity (scalable)

THE SUCCESS THAT WASN'T SUSTAINABLE

As the practice crossed into seven-figure territory, it would have been easy to think I had made it. On paper, everything looked perfect. The numbers were strong. The systems were humming. The team was growing.

But behind the scenes, something else was growing too. Exhaustion. Resentment. A quiet voice inside asking: "How much longer can you keep running at this pace?" Because while I had figured out how to build a thriving practice, I hadn't yet figured out how to build a sustainable life.

The truth was, I had mastered the art of scaling a team. Now, I needed to learn how to scale myself. Not by working harder. But by working smarter. By leading differently. By finally unlearning everything hustle culture had drilled into me.

WHAT SCALING YOURSELF REALLY MEANS

The lesson I was beginning to learn—though I wouldn't fully understand it until later—is that scaling yourself isn't about doing more. It's about doing less of the wrong things so you can do more of the right things.

It means:

- **Delegating decisions**, not just tasks
- **Building systems** that don't require your presence
- **Developing people** who can handle problems without you
- **Protecting your energy** for the things only you can do
- **Saying no** to good opportunities so you can say yes to great ones

I wasn't there yet. I was still wearing my hustle like a badge of honor, still believing that my exhaustion proved my value. The awareness was growing.

And that lesson? It would change everything.

THE DELEGATION LADDER

Most managers delegate tasks. Great leaders delegate authority. Here's how to climb from one to the other:

LEVEL 1: TASK DELEGATION

"Do exactly this, exactly this way."

- You decide what and how
- They execute your plan

- You check the work
- Good for: New employees, high-stakes situations

LEVEL 2: METHOD DELEGATION

"Here's the outcome I need. Here's generally how to get there."

- You decide what, they have input on how
- They execute with guidance
- You spot-check results
- Good for: Developing employees, medium-stakes situations

LEVEL 3: OUTCOME DELEGATION

"Here's the result I need. Figure out how to get there."

- You decide what, they decide how
- They execute independently
- You review outcomes, not process
- Good for: Proven employees, lower-stakes situations

LEVEL 4: AUTHORITY DELEGATION

"This area is yours. Make the decisions. Tell me what I need to know."

- They decide what and how
- They execute and adjust
- You stay informed but don't approve
- Good for: Your best people, areas where they're stronger than you

THE GOAL:

Move as many responsibilities as possible to Level 3 and 4. That's how you stop being the bottleneck. That's how you scale yourself without burning out.

THE FRAMEWORK THAT WOULD COME LATER

That frustration with training someone who couldn't—or wouldn't—learn case presentation didn't just teach me about team building. It sparked something bigger.

I started thinking: What if there was a way to break this down? What if case presentation wasn't some mystical skill that only a few people were born with? What if it could be taught in steps—simple, layered steps that anyone willing to put in the effort could follow?

The Bagel Method™ was beginning to form in my mind, though I didn't call it that yet. It would take more experiences, more frustrations, more trial and error before it became a real framework. But the question was already there: How do you make the complex simple enough that anyone can learn it?

That question would eventually become one of the most valuable things I'd ever teach.

Next, in Chapter 10, I'll share why I finally had to unlearn hustle culture to level up—how wearing exhaustion like a badge of honor almost cost me everything, and the unexpected invitation that forced me to become more than just an office manager.

Think about your current front office team. Do you have a balance of "relationship builders" and "financial closers"? Are you pouring your energy into growing the right people—or trying to change people who don't want to change? What's one small step you can take this month to strengthen your team for the future? And be honest: are you the bottleneck? What would break if you disappeared for two weeks?

CHAPTER 10

THE STAGE YOU'RE ALREADY BUILDING

Sometimes you don't find the stage. You look up and realize you've been building it all along.

If there's one thing I was good at, it was working. First one in, last one out. I skipped breaks, skipped birthdays, said yes when I should've said "that's not my role." I wore my exhaustion like proof of my value. Until one day I couldn't.

Even though the practice was flourishing, I knew the grind that had built it wasn't going to build my life. Something had to change. And then something did—though not in the way I expected.

THE HUSTLE TRAP

There's a dangerous lie embedded in workplace culture: that exhaustion equals value, that being busy means being important, that sacrificing everything proves your commitment. Here's the truth about the hustle trap—and how to escape it.

The Hustle Trap Beliefs:

- "If I work harder than everyone else, I'll get ahead"
- "Taking breaks means I'm not committed"
- "Being irreplaceable is job security"
- "Rest is for people who don't want it badly enough"
- "I'll slow down when I've made it"

The Reality:

- Diminishing returns set in after 50 hours per week—you work more but accomplish less
- Chronic exhaustion destroys decision-making quality
- Being indispensable means you can never advance (who would replace you?)
- Rest isn't the opposite of productivity—it's the foundation of it
- "When I've made it" never arrives; the goalpost keeps moving

By this point, the periodontist and I had developed a real partnership. He trusted me with the operations, and I'd delivered results that exceeded both our expectations. But what happened next caught me completely off guard.

He had built a name for himself in the dental world as what's known as a Key Opinion Leader. On top of practicing dentistry, he was speaking—traveling across the country and eventually the world—lecturing to rooms full of dentists about advanced procedures, new technologies, and the future of the profession. I'd seen him prepare for these events, watched him refine his presentations, knew the reputation he'd built. It was a world that felt entirely separate from mine.

So, when he suddenly suggested I join him on stage, I genuinely didn't understand what he meant at first. I froze. Speak? Me? In front of dentists?

My first thought was, *What in the world would I even talk about?* My second thought was, *Who wants to hear from a dental office manager?* In a profession built around clinical expertise and advanced degrees, what could someone like me possibly offer to a room full of doctors?

But deep down, I knew better. I knew that if you're ever given a new opportunity—especially one that scares you—you take it. You don't wait for the fear to subside. You don't overthink until the window closes. You grab it by the horns and go all in, figuring out the details on the other side of yes.

So, I said yes. And just like that, I was forced to rethink who I was.

THE "SAY YES FIRST" FRAMEWORK

Some of the best opportunities in your career will scare you. They'll feel too big, too soon, too far outside your comfort zone. Here's how to recognize the ones worth grabbing—and how to survive after you say yes.

Opportunities Worth the Fear:

- They stretch your identity, not just your skills
- Someone you respect believes you can do it
- The worst-case scenario is survivable (embarrassment, not disaster)
- You'll regret not trying more than you'll regret failing
- They open doors to rooms you can't currently enter

Opportunities to Decline:

- They compromise your values or integrity
- The person offering doesn't have your best interests in mind
- Success requires you to be someone you're not
- The timing genuinely threatens other critical priorities
- Your gut says no and you can't articulate why it should say yes

The "Yes First" Survival Plan:

1. Say yes before your fear talks you out of it
2. Immediately tell someone who will hold you accountable
3. Break the scary thing into smaller, manageable pieces
4. Find someone who's done it before and ask for advice

5. Prepare relentlessly—confidence comes from preparation

6. Accept that your first attempt won't be perfect

7. Debrief afterward: What worked? What would you change?

The Growth Formula:

Comfort zone + scary opportunity + yes = new comfort zone. Repeat indefinitely.

FROM THE FRONT DESK TO THE FRONT OF THE ROOM

We did a few events together, and with every one, I grew more confident. I created lectures focused on dental insurance and coding—topics most people avoided like the plague. But I leaned into them precisely because I had lived them. Every denied claim I'd fought, every narrative I'd written, every billing puzzle I'd solved had prepared me for this moment without my realizing it.

I talked about the codes that get missed, the narratives that get denied, the billing strategies that helped practices actually get paid for the work they did. These weren't theoretical concepts I'd read about in a textbook—they were lessons I'd learned through years of doing the work, often the hard way.

> ☯ *Manager Musings*
>
> *"The things that feel obvious to you—the hard-won lessons, the shortcuts you've discovered, the mistakes you've learned to avoid—those are exactly what someone else desperately needs to hear."*

And I realized something powerful: people didn't just want to hear what I knew. They needed to. My story, my knowledge, my perspective as a manager—it mattered. It gave people hope, shortcuts, and real-world tools they could use immediately. Dentists who had spent years in clinical training were hungry for the operational knowledge that someone like me had accumulated through sheer necessity.

That was the first time I truly saw myself as more than just a manager. I was a voice. A teacher. A leader. The same skills that had made me effective behind the front desk—communication, problem-solving, translating complexity into clarity—were exactly what made me effective in front of a room.

FINDING YOUR VOICE: WHAT YOU KNOW THAT OTHERS NEED

You have expertise others would pay to learn. The challenge is recognizing it—because the things you know well feel obvious to you. Here's how to identify your unique knowledge and start sharing it.

The Expertise Blindness Problem:

What's second nature to you is a revelation to someone else. You've forgotten how hard it was to learn what you now do automatically. That "obvious" knowledge is exactly what people need.

Identifying Your Hidden Expertise:

Ask yourself:

- What do people always ask me about?
- What mistakes do I see others making that I've learned to avoid?
- What did I struggle with early in my career that I've now mastered?
- What do I do differently than most people in my role?
- What problems can I solve in minutes that take others hours?

Packaging Your Knowledge:

Once you identify your expertise, consider how to share it:

- Writing: Articles, LinkedIn posts, internal documentation

- Speaking: Lunch-and-learns, conference presentations, team trainings

- Teaching: Mentoring, creating training materials, online courses

- Consulting: Advising other practices on your area of strength

The Imposter Syndrome Antidote:

You don't need to know everything to teach something. You just need to know more than the person you're helping—or have a perspective they haven't considered. Start where you are.

FROM LECTURES TO NATIONAL RECOGNITION

Not long after I started speaking, I got a phone call I'll never forget. It was the vice president of PennWell Corporation, the publisher behind DentistryIQ—one of the dental industry's most prominent media platforms. He asked if I'd be interested in helping spearhead a brand-new front office section on their website, dedicated specifically to dental office managers and assistants.

They wanted to call it the Dental Office Manager and Assisting Digest. And they wanted me to help lead it. I said yes before he could even finish his pitch.

I knew what it felt like to be the invisible engine behind a successful practice. If I could create a resource that made someone else's journey easier—that gave them tools or hope or just the knowledge that someone understood—then I had to do it.

So I started writing. Article after article. Every denied claim I'd ever appealed, every billing strategy I'd figured out through trial and error—it all became content that could help someone else skip the learning curve I'd endured.

BUILDING YOUR PLATFORM: FROM PRACTITIONER TO THOUGHT LEADER

The path from "person who does the work" to "person who teaches the work" isn't as far as you think. Here's the roadmap.

Stage 1: Document Your Expertise

- Start keeping notes on problems you solve
- Save templates, scripts, and processes that work
- Track results so you can speak to outcomes, not just activities
- Collect stories that illustrate your points

Stage 2: Share Internally First

- Offer to train new hires
- Create documentation for your team
- Present at staff meetings
- Volunteer to lead projects that showcase your knowledge

Stage 3: Expand Your Reach

- Write for industry publications (they're always looking for content)
- Comment thoughtfully on LinkedIn posts in your field
- Attend conferences and introduce yourself to speakers
- Join professional associations and volunteer for committees

Stage 4: Create Your Own Platform

- Start a blog, newsletter, or social media presence
- Develop a signature talk or workshop

- Build an email list of people interested in your expertise

- Consider a podcast, YouTube channel, or online course

The Patience Required:

This takes years, not months. Most "overnight successes" have been building for a decade. Start now, stay consistent, and let compound interest do its work.

The Authenticity Requirement:

People can smell fake expertise from miles away. Teach what you've actually done. Share real stories, including failures. Your credibility comes from experience, not from pretending to have all the answers.

WHY YOUR VOICE MATTERS

This chapter of my life taught me something I want you to hear: You don't have to wait for a title, a stage, or an invitation to start making an impact. You already have a story. Someone out there needs to hear what you've learned.

🎨 *Manager Musings*

"You don't have to shout to be heard. You just have to speak up—and speak from where you've been."

The speaking, the writing, the growing recognition—none of it would have happened if I'd kept my head down and just kept grinding. Sometimes you have to look up from the work to see what the work has made you capable of. Sometimes it takes someone else to hold up a mirror and show you who you've become.

That periodontist saw something in me before I saw it in myself. Just like Mary had, years earlier. And if this book can do that for even one of you—hold up that mirror—then it was worth writing.

THE LEADERSHIP YOU ALREADY HAVE

You don't need permission to lead. You don't need a title. You don't need someone to tap you on the shoulder and declare you ready. Leadership is a choice you make—usually long before anyone else recognizes it.

LEADERSHIP WITHOUT A TITLE:

- Solving problems before being asked
- Helping colleagues without keeping score
- Speaking up when something isn't right
- Taking responsibility when things go wrong
- Sharing knowledge instead of hoarding it
- Making decisions when everyone else is waiting

Many people spend their careers waiting for someone to tell them they're ready. They wait for the promotion, the title, the invitation. But here's the secret: the people who get those things are the ones who started acting like leaders before they had the label.

You don't need a stage to have a platform. Your platform is the team you work with every day, the patients you serve, the problems you solve, the example you set, and the knowledge you share.

What would change if you stopped waiting for permission and started leading today? Not in dramatic ways—in small, consistent ones. Speak up in the next meeting. Help the struggling coworker. Document that process you've figured out. Share that insight you've been sitting on.

Leadership is a muscle. The more you use it, the stronger it gets.

Next, in Chapter 11, I'll share how I built a practice that could finally run without me—what it took to systematize everything I'd learned, and why letting go of control was the hardest leadership lesson of all.

JOURNAL PROMPT:

What expertise do you have that feels "obvious" to you but could be valuable to others? What would happen if you stopped waiting for permission and started sharing what you know?

____

____

____

____

____

____

____

____

____

____

____

CHAPTER 11

BUILDING A PRACTICE THAT RUNS WITHOUT YOU

The ultimate test of leadership isn't how things run when you're there. It's what happens when you're not.

Today, as I write this book, I still manage the same dental practice. But the way I manage it—and the way the practice runs—looks very different from the early days.

The practice doesn't depend on me for survival anymore. It's built to thrive whether I'm physically there or not. And that's exactly how I designed it. Because real leadership isn't about being needed every minute—it's about building something strong enough that it doesn't crumble in your absence.

But here's the part that might surprise you: even now, with a practice that can run without me, I choose to stay. Because I remember how it felt when I left my first office—how Mary must have felt when I moved on. Loyalty matters. And no matter how far I've come, I never want to lose touch with what it really means to manage a dental practice.

The goal was never to escape the work. The goal was to transform it from something that trapped me into something that freed me.

THE FIRST STEP WAS LETTING GO

Letting go of control didn't come easy. When you've built something with your own hands—when you've poured years of blood, sweat, and missed lunches into making something work—it's hard to loosen your grip. Every instinct tells you that you're the only one who can do it right, that delegation is just another word for disappointment waiting to happen.

But I realized early on that if I wanted the practice to grow bigger than me, I had to stop being the bottleneck. The same dedication that had built this place was now holding it back. As long as everything flowed through me, we could only grow as far as my own capacity—and I was already stretched to the breaking point.

So I started small. I documented everything. Not just the obvious stuff, but the countless small decisions I made on autopilot every day. How we handle new patient calls—the exact words we use, the information we gather, the way we set expectations. How we verify insurance and present treatment plans. How we follow up on unscheduled treatment. What to check every morning, mid-day, and before closing.

It wasn't just about writing it down. It was about transferring knowledge, not keeping it locked in my head. For years, I'd been the keeper of institutional wisdom—the person who knew why we did things a certain way, what had gone wrong before, which shortcuts actually worked. All of that knowledge was locked in my head, which meant the practice was only as resilient as my presence.

Building a playbook the whole team could rely on changed everything. It meant that when questions came up, there was somewhere to look besides my office door. It meant that new hires could get up to speed faster because the information wasn't scattered across a dozen different brains. It meant that I could finally step away without the whole thing grinding to a halt.

THE DOCUMENTATION DISCIPLINE

Most managers know they should document their systems. Few actually do it—and even fewer do it well. Here's how to create documentation that actually gets used.

What to Document First:

Start with the processes that would cause the most chaos if you disappeared tomorrow. Usually that means:

- How you answer the phone (exact scripts, what information to capture)

- How you handle new patients from first call to first appointment

- How you verify insurance and explain benefits

- How you present treatment plans and discuss finances

- How you handle end-of-day reconciliation
- How you open and close the office

The Documentation Format That Works:

- Step-by-step instructions, not paragraphs of explanation
- Screenshots where applicable
- "If/then" decision trees for common variations
- Examples of what good looks like
- Common mistakes and how to avoid them

The Maintenance Reality:

Documentation is never "done." Build in a quarterly review to update what's changed. Better yet, make it part of someone's job description to keep the playbook current.

The Test:

Could someone with basic intelligence but zero dental experience follow your documentation and get it mostly right? If not, it's not detailed enough.

GROWING THE TEAM WITH PURPOSE

At first, it was just me and one front desk receptionist. We did it all—scheduling, insurance, billing, patient check-ins, treatment coordination—every task on every checklist. It was exhausting but manageable when the practice was small. We knew everything, handled everything, and kept it all in our heads.

But as the practice grew, I knew that model wouldn't be sustainable. We needed more than just additional hands—we needed structure. We needed defined roles based on people's real strengths, not just warm bodies filling seats.

So I built a team of four, each with clear responsibilities. The front desk receptionist focused on first impressions, scheduling, and patient flow—the face of the practice, the voice on the phone, the person who set the tone for every patient interaction.

The billing and insurance coordinator managed claims, payments, and insurance appeals—the financial backbone that kept revenue flowing. The insurance and clinical support coordinator handled verifications and provided chairside support when needed—the bridge between the front office and the clinical team. And I stayed on as office manager, overseeing operations, financials, leadership, and case acceptance.

I didn't just hire and hope. I observed carefully—watched where each person naturally excelled, noticed what tasks energized them versus what drained them—and then created job descriptions tailored to amplify their strengths. It's tempting to write a job description first and then try to squeeze people into it. But I found that the opposite approach worked better: watch what people are actually good at, then formalize it.

> ✒ **Manager Musings**
>
> *"Don't write the job description and then find the person. Watch the person and then write the job description around their strengths. You'll get a team that actually wants to show up."*

Sustainable practice flow doesn't happen by accident. It happens when you design the structure intentionally, matching the right people to the right responsibilities.

DESIGNING YOUR TEAM STRUCTURE

Building a team isn't just about headcount—it's about creating structure where responsibilities are clear and strengths are leveraged. Through years of trial and error, I've identified four core roles that make a front office run.

ROLE 1: FIRST IMPRESSIONS SPECIALIST (FRONT DESK/RECEPTIONIST)

- **Primary Focus:** Patient experience from first contact through check-out

- **Key Responsibilities:** Phone answering and call routing, scheduling and appointment management, patient greeting and check-in, check-out and next appointment booking, appointment confirmations and recall outreach, managing the flow of the waiting room, first-line problem-solving for patient concerns

- **Ideal Traits:** Warm and genuine personality, excellent phone presence, calm under pressure when the lobby is full and phones are ringing, organized and detail-oriented, able to multitask without losing the personal touch, naturally empathetic

ROLE 2: REVENUE SPECIALIST (BILLING/INSURANCE COORDINATOR)

- **Primary Focus:** Getting paid for the work the practice does

- **Key Responsibilities:** Claim submission and tracking, payment posting and reconciliation, insurance appeals and follow-up on denials, patient billing and collections, answering patient questions about statements and balances, identifying and resolving billing discrepancies, monitoring accounts receivable aging

- **Ideal Traits:** Detail-oriented to the point of obsession, persistent and comfortable making repeated follow-up calls, comfortable with numbers and spreadsheets, excellent follow-through on open items, able to have firm but professional collections conversations, patient when explaining complex billing to confused patients

ROLE 3: TREATMENT COORDINATOR

- **Primary Focus:** Bridging clinical recommendations and patient decisions
- **Key Responsibilities:** Insurance verification and benefits breakdown, treatment plan presentations, financial arrangement discussions, coordinating payment plans and financing options, case acceptance tracking, following up on unscheduled treatment, serving as liaison between clinical team and front office
- **Ideal Traits:** Strong communicator who can translate clinical language, confident discussing money without apologizing, genuinely curious about the clinical side of dentistry, natural relationship builder who earns patient trust, comfortable with objection handling, able to balance patient advocacy with business needs

ROLE 4: OFFICE MANAGER

- **Primary Focus:** Making sure everything and everyone works together
- **Key Responsibilities:** Oversight of all front office operations, team leadership and performance management, financial reporting and budget monitoring, problem-solving for issues that cross departmental lines, case acceptance for complex or high-value cases, systems development and process improvement, hiring and training, serving as the bridge between clinical leadership and administrative team
- **Ideal Traits:** Systems thinker who sees patterns and connections, leader who earns respect rather than demands it, accountable and willing to own mistakes, able to see both forest and trees, calm in crisis, strong communicator up and down the org chart, protective of culture while driving results

In a small practice, one person might wear two or three of these hats—and that's fine, as long as you're clear about which hat they're wearing at any given moment. The danger comes when roles blur so completely that nobody knows who owns what, and tasks fall through the cracks because everyone assumed someone else was handling it.

CROSS-TRAINING CHANGES THE GAME

As you grow, you'll naturally specialize, with generalists becoming specialists focused on one area. The key principles to remember are these: overlap between roles is okay and sometimes even healthy, but gaps are not. Every single task in your practice should have a clear owner—someone whose job it is to make sure that thing gets done. And when you're scaling, resist the urge to just add bodies. Add structure first, then fill the structure with the right people.

Once we had clear roles, I started cross-training—not because I expected everyone to master everything, but because flexibility is freedom. The front desk learned basic billing. The treatment coordinator could manage the schedule if things got slammed. When someone called out sick, we adjusted without drama.

Cross-training also built empathy. When the front desk spent a day doing billing work, they understood why certain information was critical to capture at check-in. Understanding each other's challenges made the whole team more cohesive.

THE CROSS-TRAINING MATRIX

Cross-training isn't about making everyone interchangeable, but rather ensuring no single absence creates a crisis.

Level 1: Awareness

Everyone should know what each role does, why it matters, and who to escalate to. This is basic orientation-level knowledge.

Level 2: Emergency Coverage

Each critical function should have at least one backup person who can handle the basics. Not expert-level—just enough to keep things moving for a day or two.

Level 3: True Redundancy

For mission-critical functions, train a second person to near-expert level. This takes longer but creates real resilience.

The Cross-Training Minimum:

At minimum, ensure:

- Two people can answer phones professionally
- Two people can check patients in and out
- Two people can access and navigate the schedule
- Two people understand basic insurance terminology
- Two people know how to process payments

The 80% Rule:

Don't aim for 100% competency in backup roles. 80% is enough to survive an absence without disaster. The goal is continuity, not perfection.

Implementation:

- Schedule regular "shadow days" where team members observe other roles
- Create cheat sheets for the most common tasks in each position
- Test the backup system periodically—have people actually cover other roles for a day, not just theoretically know how

EMPOWERING WITHOUT HOVERING

Having systems wasn't enough. I had to trust the people following them. This was harder than building the systems in the first place.

I stopped micromanaging. Instead of checking every detail before it went out the door, I gave ownership instead of just instructions. Instead of telling people exactly how to solve problems, I told them the outcome I needed and let them figure out the path. It felt uncomfortable at first—like watching someone else drive your car.

When mistakes happened—and they did happen—I didn't swoop in to fix them myself. I coached. I asked questions that helped people figure out where things went wrong. I let them struggle with solutions before offering my own. It took longer in the moment, but it built capability that paid dividends for years.

And over time, something remarkable happened. They grew. I grew. And the practice grew in ways it never could have when everything funneled through me.

I'll never forget the first time I took a full week off—and everything ran like clockwork. No fires to put out. No panicked phone calls. No disasters waiting for me when I returned. Just a thriving, self-sustaining office that had proven it didn't need me there every minute to function. That week felt like graduation—proof that I had finally built something bigger than myself.

THE EMPOWERMENT PROGRESSION

Moving from micromanagement to true empowerment doesn't happen overnight. Here's the progression that actually works.

Stage 1: Show and Tell

You do the task while they watch. Explain your thinking out loud—not just what you're doing, but why.

Stage 2: Guided Practice

They do the task while you watch. Offer guidance in real-time, but resist the urge to take over.

Stage 3: Supervised Independence

They do the task on their own, then report back. You review the outcome and provide feedback.

Stage 4: Full Ownership

They own the task entirely. They don't report unless there's a problem—and they handle most problems themselves.

The Micromanager Recovery Program:

If you've been a micromanager (like I was), here's how to step back:

1. Pick one task to fully delegate this week

2. Define the outcome you need, not the process to get there

3. Tell them you're available for questions, then actually step back

4. When they make a mistake, coach instead of taking over

5. Celebrate when they succeed without you

The Trust Equation:

Trust = Competence + Consistency + Time

You build it by giving people chances to prove themselves, acknowledging when they do, and staying patient when they're still learning.

YOUR SYSTEMS ARE YOUR LEGACY

You can't take the office with you. The title, the bonuses, the staff appreciation gifts—all of it stays behind when you move on. But you can leave behind a system. A structure. A standard that outlives you.

That's real leadership. Not being the hero who swoops in to save the day, but being the architect who designs something that stands whether you're in it or not.

Even today, I'm still managing this practice. Still choosing to stay close to the work. The difference is that now I stay because I choose to, not because everything would collapse without me.

BUILDING SYSTEMS THAT OUTLAST YOU

The systems you build today will shape the practice long after you've moved on. Here's how to create a legacy worth leaving.

What Makes a System Last:

- It's documented (not just in your head)
- Multiple people understand and can execute it
- It has built-in quality checks
- It can be updated as circumstances change
- It solves a real problem, not just a theoretical one

The Legacy Audit:

Ask yourself:

- If I left tomorrow, what would break?
- What knowledge exists only in my head?
- What processes depend on relationships only I have?
- What decisions can only I make?

Each answer reveals a gap in your systems—and an opportunity to build something more durable.

The Handoff Test:

Before you consider any system complete, test whether you can hand it off:

- Can you explain it in writing?
- Can someone else execute it without you standing over them?
- Can it survive staff turnover?
- Does it produce consistent results regardless of who's running it?

WHAT BUILDING INDEPENDENCE TAUGHT ME

Looking back, the journey from "the practice needs me every second" to "the practice runs without me" was one of the most difficult transitions of my career. It required me to confront my own ego—the part of me that liked being needed. Letting go felt like losing something, even though I was actually gaining freedom.

But here's what no one tells you: systems alone aren't enough. You can have the best forms and checklists in the world—and still lose your practice from the inside out if the people executing those systems are disengaged or just going through the motions.

Leadership isn't just about building systems. It's about building people. That's what I had to learn next.

Coming up, in Chapter 12, I'll share what they don't teach you about managing people. You'll learn why you can master insurance, numbers, and scheduling, but none of it matters if you can't lead the human beings on your team through their emotions, expectations, and silent battles.

What's one daily process in your office that only you know how to do? What would happen if you weren't there tomorrow? What's one system you could start building today that would create more freedom—and stronger leadership—for your future self?

CHAPTER 12

THE PART OF LEADERSHIP NOBODY WARNS YOU ABOUT

You can master insurance, numbers, and scheduling—but if you can't manage people, none of it will matter.

When I first started in dental, no one handed me a manual on how to manage people. They taught me how to run reports and file claims. No one said, "Here's how you deal with a front desk assistant crying in the bathroom because she feels undervalued." Or, "Here's what to say when a doctor undermines you in front of the staff."

The skills that get you promoted are rarely the skills you need once you're actually in charge. You get the title because you're good at systems. Then you discover the job is mostly about navigating human beings who don't come with user manuals.

So, I learned by doing—through trial, error, and a whole lot of deep breaths.

MANAGING PERSONALITIES, NOT JUST POSITIONS

Every person on your team comes with their own story. Their own habits. Their own pride, insecurities, trauma, and expectations. Some want to be left alone; give them a task, get out of their way, and they'll deliver. Others need constant affirmation; they're capable, but they wilt without regular encouragement. Some take criticism well, absorbing feedback as fuel for growth. Others take it as a personal attack, no matter how carefully you phrase it.

You can't lead everyone the same way. And that's what makes management genuinely hard. It's not the task list that breaks you—it's the translation. How do you say what needs to be said in a way this particular person can actually hear it? The same feedback that motivates one team member will devastate another. The management style that feels supportive to someone who craves structure will feel suffocating to someone who needs autonomy. There's no universal approach that works for everyone.

I learned to adjust my approach without compromising on expectations. That's the balance real leadership requires. You adapt your communication style, your feedback timing, your level of direct versus indirect guidance—but you never compromise on the actual expectations. The standard stays the same. The delivery flexes based on who you're talking to.

THE PERSONALITY-BASED LEADERSHIP GRID

Understanding how different team members need to be led transforms your effectiveness. Here's a framework for adapting your approach while maintaining consistent standards.

THE INDEPENDENT ACHIEVER

- **What they need:** Clear goals and then space to execute

- **What drains them:** Micromanagement, excessive check-ins, being forced to collaborate when they could go faster alone

- **How to lead them:** Define the outcome, set the deadline, get out of the way. Check in briefly, celebrate results, skip the hand-holding.

- **How to give feedback:** Direct and concise. They respect efficiency—don't bury the message in pleasantries.

THE AFFIRMATION SEEKER

- **What they need:** Regular acknowledgment that they're doing well

- **What drains them:** Silence (which they interpret as disapproval), criticism without context, feeling invisible

- **How to lead them:** Frequent short check-ins, verbal recognition for good work, explicit reassurance when they're on track

- **How to give feedback:** Sandwich it—genuine praise, constructive feedback, genuine encouragement. They need to know the relationship is intact.

THE PROCESSOR

- **What they need:** Time to think before responding, written instructions they can reference, predictability
- **What drains them:** Being put on the spot, rapid-fire changes, verbal-only instructions
- **How to lead them:** Give advance notice when possible, follow up conversations with written summaries, allow silence after asking questions
- **How to give feedback:** In writing first, then discuss. Let them process before expecting a response.

THE CHALLENGER

- **What they need:** To understand the "why," opportunity to push back, intellectual engagement
- **What drains them:** "Because I said so" leadership, decisions that seem arbitrary, being treated as just an executor
- **How to lead them:** Explain your reasoning, invite their perspective, let them argue (respectfully) before finalizing
- **How to give feedback:** Frame it as problem-solving together. "Here's what I'm seeing—what's your take?"

Adapting your style isn't about being fake or manipulative but recognizing that effective communication means speaking in a language the other person can receive. The message stays consistent—the delivery adapts.

THE LONELINESS IN THE MIDDLE

Even for the savviest practice managers, office politics are hard to prepare for. You can't expect how cliques form over birthday cake drama, group texts, and who got left out of the lunch order. About how team members sometimes bond against leadership, not with it. The petty stuff that seems insignificant until, suddenly, it isn't.

And when you're the one expected to hold it all together, it can get lonely. You're not quite "one of them" anymore. The easy camaraderie you might have had as a peer shifts the moment you become responsible for their performance reviews, their schedules, their accountability. But you're also not the doctor or the owner. You don't have final authority. You can't make unilateral decisions about raises or terminations or major policy changes.

You're the buffer. The translator. The therapist. The enforcer. All in one body, sometimes all in the same hour. You absorb complaints from the staff about the doctor. You absorb complaints from the doctor about the staff. You're expected to fix problems without the authority to actually change the underlying conditions creating those problems.

And no, it's not fair. But it is reality.

> ### ⏣ *Manager Musings*
>
> *"Managing people means showing up with consistency— even when you feel like you're managing chaos."*

The isolation is something most managers don't talk about, but every manager feels. You can't fully vent to your team— that would undermine your authority. You often can't fully vent to the doctor—that might make you look incapable. Finding your support system outside the office becomes essential. Other office managers who understand. A mentor who's been through it. Somewhere to be human, because the role requires you to be superhuman more often than is sustainable.

THE CONVERSATIONS NO ONE WANTS TO HAVE

You can't manage people without confrontation. And most managers avoid it. We dance around the issue, write emails with so much softening language that the message gets lost, and hope it gets better on its own.

But avoiding tough conversations creates a culture of silence—and silence creates resentment. Problems don't dissolve with time. They calcify. They become "just the way things are." They poison the water so slowly that everyone gets used to the taste.

The assistant who keeps walking in late? Every day you don't say something, you're communicating that punctuality is optional. The front desk person who's checked out emotionally? That disengagement is contagious.

The key is this: lead with clarity and compassion simultaneously. You don't have to be cruel. But you absolutely have to be clear.

HOW TO INITIATE A DIFFICULT CONVERSATION

Most managers avoid hard conversations because they don't know how to have them without damaging the relationship. But there's a structure that works.

Before you speak: Get clear on the specific behavior—not personality, not attitude. "You rolled your eyes during the morning huddle" is observable. "You have a bad attitude" isn't. Know the impact of the behavior and what outcome you need.

Open with observation, not accusation: "I've noticed you've been arriving ten to fifteen minutes late the past two weeks."

Not: "You're always late and it's disrespectful." The first states a fact. The second triggers defensiveness.

Connect behavior to consequences: "When you arrive late, Sarah has to cover the phones alone during our busiest time. Patients wait longer, and she's stressed before the day starts." Most people don't think through the ripple effects of their actions.

Make space for their side: "Help me understand what's going on." Then actually listen. There may be context you don't have.

Be crystal clear about what needs to change: "Going forward, I need you here and ready to work at 8:00. Not walking in at 8:00—ready to work." Don't apologize for having standards. Clarity is kindness.

Establish accountability: "Let's check in on this in two weeks." Then actually follow up. This is where most managers fail—they have the conversation, feel relieved, and never mention it again until the behavior resurfaces.

The goal isn't punishment. It's giving people the information they need to succeed.

WHEN FRIENDSHIP CROSSES THE LINE

There will be days when you doubt yourself. Days when someone quits and you wonder if it's your fault. Days when the owner questions your decisions. Days when the team resents you for enforcing the very policies they asked you to create.

And sometimes, the hardest thing to do is pull back.

> ✏️ *Manager Musings*
>
> *"A team can like you, laugh with you, even trust you—but if they don't respect you, your leadership won't last."*

I remember getting too close to a front desk receptionist. We bonded quickly—laughed together, shared personal stories. The line between professional and personal blurred in a way that felt natural. We weren't just coworkers anymore. We were friends.

But over time, the dynamic shifted. She started speaking to me in ways that felt dismissive—like I wasn't her supervisor anymore, just someone she could roll her eyes at. The friendship had eroded the authority I needed to do my job. And that's when I realized: there's no easy way to "unfriend" someone in real life.

I had to pull back. Re-establish boundaries that I had let dissolve. Make clear that while I cared about her as a person, our working relationship needed to function within certain parameters. It wasn't pretty. It caused tension. It hurt both of us. But it had to be done.

Because I couldn't lead a team that didn't respect my position—and respect starts with the boundaries I set. I was the one who had let them blur. It was my responsibility to rebuild them.

I still wrestled with guilt afterward. Still wondered if I could have handled it differently, maintained the friendship while recovering the professional distance. But I learned something important: being liked can never come at the cost of being respected. When you have to choose—and eventually you will have to choose—respect has to win.

THE MANAGER-STAFF BOUNDARY FRAMEWORK

Too distant and you lose connection. Too close and you lose authority. Here's how to find the middle.

The Test Questions:

Before deepening a friendship with a team member, ask yourself:

- Could I give this person critical feedback tomorrow without it being awkward?

- Could I enforce a policy they didn't like without them taking it personally?

- If I had to let them go, would our personal relationship compromise that decision?

If You've Already Crossed the Line:

Have a private conversation. "I've realized I need to re-establish some professional boundaries. It's not about our friendship—it's about my ability to lead effectively." Then be consistent. You can be friendly without being friends.

THE BIGGER REALIZATION

Even with all the lessons, all the leadership scars—there came a point when I realized something: Leading one practice wasn't enough.

Managers like me were everywhere. In every town. In every office. Fighting the same silent battles. Feeling the same loneliness. Figuring everything out alone because no one had bothered to write down what actually works.

What if I could help them skip some of the pain I'd gone through?

That question would eventually lead me somewhere I never expected. But first, I had more to learn about culture—specifically, what happens when you have to rebuild it from the inside out.

Next, in Chapter 13, I'll share what happens when culture starts breaking down—how to confront the tensions you've been avoiding, why keeping toxic employees costs you your best people, and the daily practice that separates workplaces people tolerate from workplaces people fight to stay in.

Think about the team member who's hardest for you to lead. What's different about their personality that makes your usual approach less effective? What would change if you adapted your style to speak their language—without lowering your standards? And be honest: is there a relationship on your team where the boundaries have blurred in ways that might be affecting your authority?

CHAPTER 13

CULTURE IS A DAILY PRACTICE

You can't fix culture with snacks and smiles. You fix it by doing the real, unglamorous work of leading with reliability.

You know when the culture in your office is off. You feel it before you can name it. The air is heavier. Conversations are shorter. People stop greeting each other in the morning—not a dramatic avoidance, just an absence of warmth that used to be automatic. The team gets really good at pretending everything's fine, which is its own kind of exhausting performance.

And if you're the manager, you feel it first. Because you're the one everyone vents to. You're the one expected to fix it. And you're the one silently asking: "Where do I even begin?"

YOU CAN'T CHANGE WHAT YOU DON'T CONFRONT

Culture isn't defined by the values poster in your breakroom. It's defined by what you tolerate when no one's looking.

I had a front desk receptionist and a dental assistant who could never seem to get along. It wasn't big, screaming fights—nothing that dramatic. It was the little things: the eye rolls when one mentioned the other's name, the passive-aggressive comments disguised as jokes, the tension patients could feel even if they didn't know why. The energy shifted whenever they were in the same room.

And for a while, I tolerated too much. I thought if I just stayed focused on the bigger goals—collections, case acceptance, scheduling—the little dramas would work themselves out. I assumed that they should be able to handle their own interpersonal issues and hoped that if I ignored the tension, it would eventually dissolve on its own. I told myself, "They're adults," and looked the other way.

Unfortunately, they didn't want to act like adults. And before long, the tension leaked into the team, into the patient experience, and eventually into the culture itself. Other staff members started taking sides. The office that had felt unified began to fracture along invisible lines.

There was no more looking the other way; I had to step in. I didn't expect them to become best friends forever—that wasn't realistic, and it wasn't the goal. But I needed them to be professional, cordial, and protect the bigger thing we were all building.

I pulled them aside—not together at first, but individually—to understand each perspective without the defensiveness that comes from being outnumbered. Then I brought them together and addressed it head-on.

"You don't have to like each other outside of work," I told them. "You don't have to hang out after hours or become friends. But inside these walls, we treat each other with respect. We work together. We support the mission. That's not optional—it's the price of being on this team."

> ### ☺ *Manager Musings*
>
> *"Conflict you ignore doesn't dissolve—it hardens into culture."*

Both were defensive at first, convinced the other was entirely at fault. But I didn't let them relitigate every grievance. I kept the focus forward: What does professional behavior look like going forward?

The tension didn't disappear overnight. But naming it—calling out what everyone could feel but no one was addressing—broke the spell. They didn't become friends, but they became functional. The eye rolls stopped. The patients stopped feeling that unnamed tension.

THE CULTURE CONFRONTATION FRAMEWORK

Addressing cultural issues feels risky—what if you make it worse? Here's how to confront problems without creating bigger ones.

Before the Confrontation:

- Get clear on the specific behaviors you're addressing (not personalities, not assumptions about motives)

- Gather perspectives from multiple sources if possible

- Identify what "success" looks like—what behavior change do you actually need?

- Choose a private setting where emotions can be expressed without an audience

The Individual Conversations First:

Before bringing conflicting parties together, meet with each separately:

- "I've noticed some tension between you and [name]. Help me understand your perspective."

- Let them vent. Don't agree or disagree—just listen.

- Identify what they need to move forward (often it's just being heard)

The Joint Conversation: When you bring them together:

- Set ground rules: no interrupting, no relitigating the past, focus on solutions

- State the impact clearly: "This tension is affecting the team and our patients"

- Ask each person what they need from the other (specific behaviors, not personality changes)

- Get commitments to specific changes

- Set a follow-up date to check progress

The Non-Negotiable Statement:

Be prepared to draw the line clearly: "You don't have to be friends. You do have to be professional. If this continues to affect our team and patients, I'll have to make decisions neither of us wants to make."

After the Confrontation:

- Follow up individually within a week

- Acknowledge any improvement you observe

- Address backsliding immediately—don't let it re-establish

RESETTING EXPECTATIONS THAT ACTUALLY STICK

Once I started confronting issues head-on, I realized something: half the problems in our culture existed because expectations had never been clearly set—or had eroded over time. People weren't being difficult on purpose. They genuinely didn't know what "professional" was supposed to look like because no one had defined it recently.

Resetting expectations didn't mean dropping a memo and hoping for miracles. It meant real conversations. Sitting down with the team. Re-aligning our values. Redefining what "professional" looks like in concrete, observable terms. Making it crystal clear what's no longer acceptable—not as a threat, but as a clarification.

You can't change culture in a day. But you can start that day with a new standard.

The key is making expectations specific enough to be observable. "Be more professional" is useless—everyone thinks they're already being professional. "Greet every patient within thirty seconds of them walking in the door" is specific. "Don't discuss coworkers negatively when they're not present" is specific. "When you have a problem with someone, address it directly with them or bring it to me—don't vent to the rest of the team" is specific.

I also learned that resetting expectations works best when you explain the "why" behind them. People will follow rules they understand. They'll resist rules that feel arbitrary. Taking ten minutes to explain how a behavior affects patient experience, team morale, or operational efficiency transforms compliance into buy-in.

WHEN YOU LOSE PEOPLE, YOU MAKE ROOM FOR THE RIGHT ONES

Not everyone is meant to grow with you. And every toxic employee you keep? They're not just staying—they're pushing the good ones out the door.

In my two decades in dental management, I've seen it all. Loyal team members who became family. Toxic employees who poisoned the culture quietly, one eye roll or complaint at a time. People who stayed through the hard seasons. And others who left for bigger and better things.

The truth is that you don't always get to control who stays loyal or who leaves. People grow. People move on. That's not failure—that's life. But here's what you do get to control: how you elevate the ones who are loyal to you. How you invest in the people who make your life easier, your team stronger, and your culture better.

Because the real practice builders—the ones who show up, adapt, problem-solve, and stay aligned with your mission—they deserve to be seen. They deserve to be valued. And if you don't show them that, someone else will.

One thing that changed how I lead was learning about love languages—the simple truth that people crave different kinds of appreciation. Some need words of affirmation. Some need small gifts. Some need acts of service. Some just need time and attention. If you've never studied love languages, start. Because if you understand how someone needs to feel appreciated, you can tailor your recognition in ways that actually land—and the impact will be bigger than you realize.

There was a team member who wasn't just good at her job—she was loyal. She was the one staying late when it mattered. Helping the newer staff find their footing. Carrying the emotional load when others would have crumbled. But her salary wasn't keeping up. And it wasn't because we didn't value her—it was because the practice genuinely didn't have the budget flexibility at the time.

> ### 🧠 *Manager Musings*
>
> *"The ones who stay and build with you aren't just employees. They're part of your legacy. Invest accordingly."*

I knew we couldn't offer her the raise she deserved right away. But I also knew we couldn't afford to lose her. So I made it my mission to recognize her in the way she needed most. I celebrated her wins publicly. I bought her lunch when she crushed a tough collection month. I made sure she knew—loud and clear—that her work mattered. That she mattered.

It wasn't perfect. It wasn't always enough. But it kept her motivated through the tough seasons. Because sometimes appreciation isn't about grand gestures. It's about consistent, real, personal leadership.

THE RETENTION INVESTMENT FRAMEWORK

Keeping your best people isn't just about money—it's about making them feel valued in ways that matter to them.

Identify Your Keepers: Who would hurt most to lose? Not just skill-wise, but culturally. Those are your retention priorities.

Discover Their Language: How does each person feel appreciated? Words of recognition? Small gifts? Help with their workload? Time and genuine interest in their life? Tailor your appreciation to land.

When Money Isn't Available: Be honest about the constraints. Ask what else would make them feel valued. Over-invest in recognition in the meantime. Make a timeline for when compensation can be revisited.

The Hard Truth: Sometimes your best efforts aren't enough. When someone loyal leaves despite your efforts, thank them, celebrate what they contributed, and let them go with grace. How you handle departures shapes how the remaining team views you.

CULTURE IS A DAILY PRACTICE—NOT A ONE-TIME FIX

When someone loyal leaves—or when you fight to keep them—it's easy to think, "Okay, we're good now. We've built the culture we want." But here's the truth: culture isn't something you build once and check off the list. It's not a banner you hang up at a team meeting. It's not a one-time bonus or a pizza party. Culture is a daily practice. A hundred little moments, multiplied by time.

It's how you respond when a patient disrespects a team member—do you have their back, or do you appease the patient at their expense? It's how you handle mistakes—privately, respectfully, and constructively, or publicly and punitively? It's how you celebrate wins, both big and small. It's how you hold the line on the values you say you believe in—even when it's uncomfortable, even when it would be easier to let it slide.

You don't just protect culture when things are easy. You protect it when it's inconvenient. When the schedule's slammed. When emotions are running high. When leadership feels like the last thing you have energy for.

I've seen it happen both ways. I've seen strong teams crumble because leadership stopped showing up daily. They stopped having the hard conversations. They stopped celebrating the little wins. They let gossip slide because they were "too busy" to deal with it. And before they knew it, the culture they had worked so hard to build was slipping through their fingers.

And I've seen struggling teams turn around because leadership recommitted daily. They kept the standards clear. They protected each other fiercely. They stayed steady—not perfect, but steady.

Culture is a living, breathing thing. You have to water it. Feed it. Protect it. Every single day. And if you do? You won't just have a better practice. You'll have a better team. A stronger community. A workplace that people actually want to stay in, fight for, and grow with.

THE DAILY CULTURE CHECKLIST

Culture isn't built in annual retreats—it's built in daily moments.

Morning: Greet every team member by name. Set the tone with your own energy—they mirror you.

Throughout the Day: Catch someone doing something right and say so. Address small issues immediately instead of storing them up. Have your team's back when patients are difficult.

End of Day: Thank the team for something specific. Note any cultural issues to address tomorrow.

Weekly: Celebrate at least one win publicly. Address any brewing tensions before they harden.

None of these actions is dramatic. But multiplied by days, weeks, and months, they become the culture.

LEADING LIKE AN OWNER—EVEN WHEN YOU'RE NOT

You don't get to step into leadership halfway. You either own the tone—or someone else will set it for you.

It took me a while to learn that lesson. There were times when I thought, "I'm just the office manager. It's not my name on the building. It's not my license on the line." That thinking let me off the hook for things I should have addressed. It gave me an excuse to defer, to wait for someone else to handle it, to limit my own authority before anyone else did. But culture doesn't care about your title—it follows the person who steps up when it matters.

One day, our front desk team member handled a patient situation in a way the periodontist disagreed with. Instead of addressing it privately, he corrected her in front of the waiting room—cold, logical, stripped of any emotional intelligence. She broke down in tears at the front desk. A patient witnessed the entire thing.

When I walked up and saw the scene—our team member crying, staff surrounding her, the patient looking on—I knew this wasn't just a bad moment. It was a cultural crisis.

I pulled the periodontist aside. Not to attack—but to lead. I explained what he hadn't seen: a patient had witnessed everything. The team was shaken. The tone he had set wasn't just about that one conversation—it was about how people would now feel coming into our practice.

I made it clear: leadership isn't just about being right. It's about protecting trust and emotional safety. That moment changed his approach. More importantly, the team saw that someone would speak up when things went wrong—even to the doctor.

Another time, one of our front desk team members was handling a call with a patient who had become verbally abusive. I could see the stress building on her face.

I walked over, asked her to hand me the phone, and stepped in. I listened. I gave the patient space to explain his frustration. But when the conversation spiraled into continued disrespect, I made a decision: I respectfully told him he was no longer welcome at our practice. We sent a certified dismissal letter, documented everything, and closed the chapter.

The truth is, leadership sometimes means absorbing the heat yourself so your team doesn't have to. Even when your title says "manager" and not "owner." Because real leadership is never about holding the highest position. It's about holding the highest standards.

THE FOUNDATION FOR EVERYTHING ELSE

After years of resets and realigning teams, I started to see something I hadn't fully appreciated. All the culture work wasn't just about creating a better workplace—it was creating the foundation for everything else.

> ☺ **Manager Musings**
>
> *"When you set the wrong tone, your team will follow it. But the good news is—you can always rewrite the script."*

When your team trusts each other, patients feel it. The same principles that built strong teams also built strong patient relationships: trust, clarity, consistency, meeting people where they are instead of where you wish they were.

And that realization would change everything about how I approached case acceptance—through something I call "The Bagel Method."

Next, in Chapter 14, I'll share how everything I learned about culture and connection came together in the patient chair—why trust comes before treatment, how to guide patients to "yes" without pressure, and "The Bagel Method" that transformed our case acceptance into something that felt natural instead of salesy.

What's one small leadership behavior you could commit to daily that would strengthen your office culture over time? What's one "bad habit" your team has picked up that you could start gently correcting today? And ask yourself honestly: when was the last time you stepped up to protect your team—even when it was uncomfortable?

CHAPTER 14

GETTING PATIENTS TO SAY "YES" TO TREATMENT (THE BAGEL METHOD™)

Patients aren't only buying treatment—they're also buying trust.

After all the leadership lessons, the culture resets, and the systems I had built, something shifted. For the first time in my career, I had the foundation in place. And that freedom let me focus on what I truly loved: talking to patients. Listening to their stories. Sharing parts of my own.

Early on, I led with facts. "You need two crowns. Your insurance pays this much. We can fit you in next week." Logical. Efficient. Ineffective. Patients would nod along, take the treatment plan, and disappear. The "think about it" patients rarely came back.

I blamed everything else at first. The insurance didn't cover enough. The patient couldn't afford it. The doctor didn't explain things well. But eventually I had to admit: the problem was the process. I was treating case presentations like checklists—items to get through efficiently—not like conversations with human beings who were nervous, confused, and looking for someone to trust.

So I changed my approach. I slowed down. I asked better questions. I used visuals instead of just describing problems. I stopped treating case presentations like transactions and started treating them like opportunities to build relationships.

> ### 🧠 *Manager Musings*
>
> *"Trust isn't a line in your treatment plan—it's the unspoken agreement that you care, you understand, and you're here to help."*

The more I leaned into connection, the more my case acceptance climbed. Not because I became a better salesperson—I actually became less "salesy." I became more human. And that's what patients wanted all along.

OFFER CONNECTION FIRST, INFORMATION SECOND

Most practices fall into the same trap I had, approaching case acceptance backwards. They lead with clinical information and financial details, then wonder why patients hesitate. It seems logical—give people the facts and let them make an informed decision. But it doesn't account for how human beings actually make decisions.

Think about the typical approach. The patient finishes their exam, and within minutes they're hearing about the treatment they need, the clinical details of the procedure, what it's going to cost, and what their insurance will or won't cover. Then comes the ask: "Would you like to schedule?" The patient, still processing a flood of information—some of it anxiety-inducing—hesitates. "Let me think about it," they say. And they mean it. They do need to think about it, because they've been given a lot of information but no real reason to feel confident in the decision.

As a result, patients feel processed, not cared for. They feel like a number moving through a system optimized for efficiency, not a person being helped through a difficult decision.

WHY TRUST COMES BEFORE TREATMENT

The trust-first approach flips this entirely. Instead of leading with information, you lead with connection. You build real rapport first—you see them as a person, not a procedure. You take time to ensure they understand what's being recommended and that they feel heard, not just informed. You address fears and concerns proactively, before those concerns become objections. You guide them through the logistics with patience instead of rushing to the finish line. And when it's time to ask for commitment, it feels natural—not pressured.

The result is dramatically different. Patients feel guided, not sold. They feel like you're on their side, helping them navigate something complicated, rather than trying to close a deal. Case acceptance goes up, but more importantly, follow-through improves. Patients who say yes actually show up for their appointments. They don't cancel at the last minute or ghost you entirely.

The psychology behind this is straightforward: patients make emotional decisions, then justify them with logic. If they don't feel safe with you—if they don't feel actually cared for—no amount of logical explanation will get them to yes. You can present the most compelling clinical case in the world, and they'll still find a reason to delay. But if they trust you, they'll follow your recommendations even when the numbers are uncomfortable. They'll find a way to make it work because they believe you're steering them right.

Before every case presentation, ask yourself one question: Does this patient feel like I genuinely care about their wellbeing, or do they feel like I'm trying to close a sale? Be honest with yourself. The answer to that question determines your outcome more than any script, any visual aid, or any financing option ever will.

But "build connection first" isn't a strategy. It's a philosophy. And philosophies don't help when you're standing in front of a patient trying to figure out what to actually say. I needed something teachable—a repeatable framework that anyone could follow.

HOW THE BAGEL METHOD™ WAS BORN

As the practice grew, I began tracking what worked. Certain words that made patients lean in. Certain timing that made decisions feel easier. Certain ways of layering information that made the complex feel simple.

I documented the patterns. Refined them. Tested them. Until one day, I realized I had created a system—a step-by-step flow for case acceptance that wasn't about pressure or sales tactics. It was about offering clarity and leading patients through their decisions with care. Layer by layer. Like building the perfect bagel.

And yeah—I named it after a bagel. Because bagels are simple. They're complete. And when they're made right? They're hard to say no to.

IT'S PERSONAL

If you remember from earlier in this book—I used to buy a single bagel every morning during those early days at my first practice. I'd eat half for breakfast. Save the other half for lunch. Because that's what I could afford while I was grinding through recall calls for minimum wage plus bonuses.

That bagel represented survival. Focus. Drive. It taught me how to stretch what I had and make it work. It was a daily reminder that I was building toward something, even when I couldn't see it yet.

And let's be real—being from New York City, I believe we have the best bagels in the world. Challenge me if you want. I'll stand by it.

The bagel means something to me. It reminds me where I started. And now, it represents how something simple—when layered right—can become transformational. Just like a great bagel is made in layers, great case acceptance is built in layers. You can't skip steps and expect it to hold together.

THE SIX LAYERS OF THE BAGEL METHOD

A great bagel is made in layers. It starts with the foundation—flour, water, yeast. Then it's shaped. Boiled. Baked. Finally, it's topped—with whatever fits best. Skip a step and the whole thing falls apart. Rush the process and you end up with something that looks like a bagel but doesn't have the substance.

Treatment acceptance is no different. You need a solid base of trust. A well-shaped explanation of the problem. A confident, clearly presented solution. And finally—your ask, topped with sincerity and confidence. Each layer builds on the one before it.

The Bagel Method™ breaks down into six layers: B.A.G.E.L.S. Each one is essential to the whole.

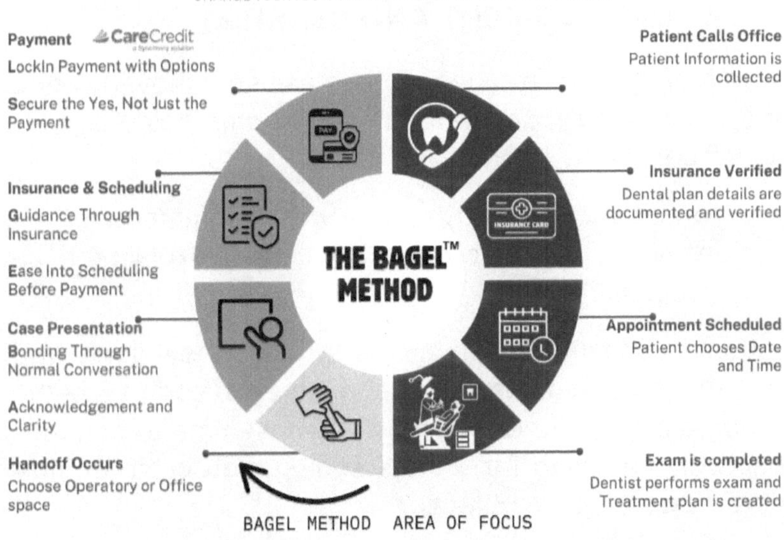

B—BONDING THROUGH NORMAL CONVERSATION

Start with a genuine human connection. Not clinical. Not financial. Simple, real connection.

"Hi, I'm Kyle—nice to meet you! How was check-in today?"

This isn't small talk for the sake of filling silence. This is the foundation everything else rests on. When a patient feels safe from the start—when they feel like they're talking to a person who sees them as a person—the whole conversation becomes easier. They're more likely to ask questions. More likely to share concerns. More likely to trust your recommendations.

If the first words out of your mouth are clinical or financial, you've already lost ground. You've signaled that this is a transaction, not a relationship. And in a transaction, the patient's job is to protect themselves—to be skeptical, to look for the catch, to say "let me think about it" as a defense mechanism.

A—ACKNOWLEDGMENT AND CLARITY

Before money, before scheduling—make sure they truly understand what was recommended. This seems obvious, but it's skipped constantly in busy practices.

"Are you clear on what treatment was recommended?" "Any questions about how it's done?" "Want me to explain the materials or process?"

Patients can't move forward with what they don't understand. And most patients won't admit they're confused—they'll just nod along and then hesitate when it's time to commit. By proactively checking for understanding, you catch confusion before it becomes an objection.

This layer is also about honoring their intelligence. You're not talking down to them or assuming they're ignorant. You're making space for questions and clarification. That respect earns their confidence.

G—GUIDANCE THROUGH INSURANCE

Insurance confusion kills case acceptance. Patients think their insurance covers more than it does, then feel blindsided by their out-of-pocket cost. That blindsided feeling turns into distrust—even though you did nothing wrong.

I always ask: "Are you familiar with how your dental plan works?"

Usually the answer is no. So I explain simply: "Dental insurance is like an allowance—not true coverage. It's capped and limited. Here's what it covers, and here's what it doesn't."

Transparency first. No confusion. No surprises. When patients understand the reality of their insurance before you present costs, the numbers feel less shocking. You've inoculated them against sticker shock by setting accurate expectations.

E—EASE INTO SCHEDULING BEFORE PAYMENT

Here's a counterintuitive move that dramatically improves case acceptance: schedule them before you ask for money.

Most practices do it backwards—they present the cost, watch the patient hesitate at the number, and then try to schedule. But now the appointment is associated with the financial pain. The patient is already in resistance mode.

Instead, lock in the commitment first. "Let's get you on the schedule—does Thursday at 2 work, or is morning better for you?" Once they've mentally committed to the appointment, the financial conversation becomes about logistics, not about whether they're moving forward.

This works because of a psychological principle called commitment and consistency. Once people make a small commitment, they're more likely to follow through with related actions. The appointment is the commitment. The payment is just the follow-through.

L—LOCK IN PAYMENT WITH OPTIONS

When you get to payment, offer structure and choice—not a single number and silence.

"You can pay in full today, or we can split it—deposit now, balance at your prep appointment, final payment at delivery. Some patients also use CareCredit for larger cases if monthly payments work better. What feels most comfortable for you?"

Always ask: "What monthly payment would feel comfortable for you?" This question transforms the conversation from "can you afford this?" to "how would you like to structure this?" It assumes the yes and focuses on the path.

Make the path easy. Remove obstacles. Your job isn't to judge what patients can afford—it's to provide options that let them say yes in a way that works for their situation.

S—SECURE THE YES, NOT JUST THE PAYMENT

End with confidence and clarity.

"You're all set—we've got you scheduled for next Thursday at 3 p.m. We'll collect your deposit today and walk you through next steps."

If they hesitate, pivot gently. Ask what's holding them back. Address concerns. But secure something—because motivation drops the second they leave the building. The patient who seems 80% ready in your office becomes 40% ready by the time they get home and start second-guessing.

This doesn't mean pressuring. It means not leaving things ambiguous. A clear next step—even if it's "let me send you some information and call you tomorrow"—is better than "just call us when you're ready."

B—Bonding Through Normal Conversation Build rapport before business. Make them feel like a person, not a procedure.

A—Acknowledgment and Clarity Confirm they understand what was recommended. Create space for questions.

G—Guidance Through Insurance Educate them on how dental insurance actually works before discussing costs.

E—Ease Into Scheduling Before Payment Lock in the appointment first. Payment becomes logistics, not decision.

L—Lock in Payment with Options Offer multiple payment structures. Ask what works for them.

S—Secure the Yes End with clarity and confidence. Don't leave it open-ended.

After each case presentation, ask yourself: Did I hit all six layers? Which one did I rush or skip? That's usually where the "let me think about it" came from.

WHY THE BAGEL METHOD™ WORKS

The Bagel Method™ isn't magic. It's psychology, structure, and real human connection—delivered in a repeatable way that anyone can learn.

It works because it honors patient fears without feeding them, breaks complex treatment into digestible steps, and treats patients like intelligent adults who deserve clarity. The best case acceptance doesn't feel like sales. It feels like help.

This works for front desk intake, hygiene handoffs, treatment coordinator presentations, and doctor-led case discussions. Anyone can learn it. You don't have to be a "natural closer." You just have to care enough to guide.

TEACHING THE BAGEL METHOD™ TO YOUR TEAM

The Bagel Method™ only works if your whole team uses it. Here's how to train them effectively.

WEEK 1: INTRODUCE THE CONCEPT

- Share the six layers and explain why each matters
- Connect it to patient psychology, not sales tactics
- Make clear this is about helping patients, not pressuring them

WEEK 2: ROLE-PLAY EACH LAYER

- Practice B (Bonding) openers until they feel natural
- Practice A (Acknowledgment) questions for checking understanding
- Practice G (Guidance) insurance explanations
- Practice E (Ease) scheduling language
- Practice L (Lock in) payment option presentations
- Practice S (Secure) confident closing statements

WEEK 3: OBSERVE AND COACH

- Watch team members in real patient interactions
- Note which layers they're hitting and which they're skipping
- Provide specific feedback after each interaction

ONGOING: HUDDLE CHECK-INS

- Review case acceptance numbers weekly
- Discuss "lost" cases—which layer broke down?
- Celebrate wins and identify what worked

COMMON TRAINING MISTAKES:

- Teaching it as a script instead of a framework (sounds robotic)
- Skipping role-play (everyone thinks they can do it until they try)
- Not following up after initial training (old habits return fast)

Every team member should be able to explain why each layer matters, not just what to say. Understanding the psychology makes the method feel natural instead of forced.

WHAT THE BAGEL METHOD™ MADE POSSIBLE

The Bagel Method™ gave our team a shared language for case acceptance. It took something that felt like an art—something only "natural salespeople" could do—and turned it into a teachable system.

Our case acceptance climbed. But more importantly, patients stopped feeling sold to and started feeling cared for. They referred friends and family. They came back for treatment they'd been putting off for years.

And it all started with a bagel.

Next, in Chapter 15, I'll show you The Bagel Method™ in action—real conversations, common mistakes, and how to handle the objections that still come up even when you do everything right.

Think about your last "let me think about it" patient. Which layer of The Bagel Method™ did you skip or rush? What would you do differently if you could replay that conversation? And be honest: do your case presentations feel like conversations, or do they feel like checklists you're trying to get through?

____

____

____

____

____

____

____

____

____

____

____

____

THE BAGEL METHOD IN ACTION

Knowing the layers is important. But mastering them happens when you use them in actual conversations—with actual patients, actual emotions, and actual doubts.

You know the system now. You understand the structure. But understanding a framework and executing it under pressure are two different things.

Patients aren't thinking, "Wow, they really bonded with me first!" They're not evaluating your technique. They're having an invisible conversation underneath the words—one you need to recognize and respond to.

They're thinking: "Do I trust this person?" "Do I feel clear and comfortable saying yes?" "Is this really necessary, or are they just trying to sell me something?"

That's the real conversation happening in every case presentation. Your job is to guide that conversation toward confidence and clarity.

In this chapter, I'll show you the Bagel Method in action through real patient scenarios, including what happens when you execute it well and what happens when you skip layers. Then we'll walk through how to practice with your team so these conversations become second nature.

A REAL PATIENT STORY: BOND FIRST, TREATMENT SECOND

I remember a patient—we'll call her Maria—who came in for a consultation on a cracked tooth. Logically, it was straightforward: she needed a crown. It wasn't optional. It wasn't complicated. The diagnosis was clear, and the treatment plan wrote itself.

But Maria was tense. Guarded. Her arms were crossed in the chair. Her answers were short and cautious. Everything about her body language said she wasn't ready to hear about crowns and costs—she was still deciding whether she could trust us at all.

Before I ever mentioned treatment, I took five minutes just talking with her. Not about teeth. About her. "How was parking today?" "What brought you to our office?" "How long have you been feeling discomfort?" Simple questions. Nothing clinical. Nothing financial. Just human conversation that signaled I saw her as a person, not a procedure.

As we talked, her body language softened. Her arms uncrossed. Her smile came back. Her voice got warmer. The tension in the room dissipated. She was still sitting in a dental office facing an expensive procedure, but she was no longer bracing for impact.

Only then did I explain the crown. Not with technical jargon— but with clarity and reassurance. I showed her what was happening with her tooth. I explained why a crown was the right solution. I made sure she understood and had space to ask questions.

By the time I asked, "Would you like to get that scheduled today?" she smiled and said, "Absolutely. Thank you for explaining it so clearly."

That's the Bagel Method working exactly as designed. The bonding came first. The trust was established before the treatment was ever discussed. By the time we got to the ask, it felt natural—like the obvious next step in a conversation between two people who understood each other.

Maria didn't say yes because I had a great script. She said yes because she felt seen, heard, and guided. The clinical and financial details mattered, but they mattered less than how the whole interaction made her feel.

WHAT HAPPENS WHEN YOU SKIP A LAYER

Now let me tell you about James. Middle-aged. Engineer. Logical thinker. Someone who valued details and clarity—exactly the kind of patient you'd think would respond well to a straightforward, facts-first approach.

James came in for a consultation on a failing tooth. The diagnosis was clear: the tooth couldn't be saved. It needed an extraction, followed by a bone graft and membrane to preserve the site for a future implant. Clinically, there was no ambiguity. The treatment plan was solid.

The doctor finished the exam and handed it off to me for case presentation. And because we were busy that day—because I was thinking about the three patients waiting and the phone that kept ringing—I rushed right into it.

"You'll need an extraction, a bone graft, and a membrane to maintain the site. Your insurance will cover part of the extraction, but not the graft or membrane. Your out-of-pocket cost will be about $2,400. We can schedule you next week if you'd like."

No real conversation. No bonding. No patient education. Just the facts—and a pretty big price tag delivered without any context or emotional preparation.

James nodded politely. Took the printout. Said he'd "think about it." We never heard from him again. Looking back, I can see exactly where I failed. I skipped almost every layer of the Bagel Method, and the result was predictable.

I skipped bonding; I didn't take time to ease his fear about losing a tooth. For James, this wasn't just clinical information. He was losing a part of his body. And I treated it like a line item.

I skipped acknowledgment and insurance guidance; I assumed he understood what a bone graft and membrane were, threw terminology at him, and then hit him with "$2,400 out of pocket" without explaining why insurance only partially covers surgical preservation.

I skipped easing into scheduling and payment options; I made money the headline instead of locking in the appointment first. I never offered CareCredit or structured payments. For all I know, James would have said yes if I'd offered to split the cost. I'll never know, because I never asked.

Skipping even one layer can cost you the entire case. Skipping several almost guarantees a no—especially when the treatment feels scary, expensive, and emotionally loaded.

It wasn't that James couldn't afford it. It was that I gave him information without giving him a reason to trust. And information without trust just creates more doubt.

☺ Manager Musings

"When patients walk out with uncertainty, it's rarely because they don't care. It's because we didn't guide them well enough."

THE LAYER BREAKDOWN: MARIA VS. JAMES

When you compare these two cases side by side, the difference becomes obvious—and instructive.

Layer	Maria (Success)	James (Failure)
B – Bonding	Took five minutes for genuine conversation before any clinical discussion	Skipped entirely—jumped straight to treatment
A –Acknowledgment	Checked understanding, showed visuals, made space for questions	Assumed understanding, used jargon without explanation
G – Guidance (Insurance)	Explained coverage clearly before presenting costs	Threw numbers without context
E – Ease into Scheduling	Scheduled first, then discussed payment	Led with cost, made money the headline
L – Lock in Payment	Offered options, asked what worked for her	No payment options discussed
S – Secure the Yes	Natural commitment after trust was built	Left with uncertainty and a printout

The treatment complexity wasn't that different. Maria's crown wasn't simpler than James's extraction and graft. The difference was entirely in how the conversation was conducted. Maria felt guided. James felt processed.

ROLE-PLAYING THE BAGEL METHOD WITH YOUR TEAM

Reading about the Bagel Method is one thing. Executing it when you're face-to-face with a nervous patient while the phone is ringing—that's another.

That's why role-playing matters. In the real world, patients don't follow scripts. They interrupt. They hesitate. They change the subject. They get nervous about money. They ask questions you weren't expecting. They shut down in ways you can't predict.

Your team needs to feel comfortable guiding the conversation naturally—no matter what comes up. And the only way to build that comfort is through practice.

Here's a simple exercise you can run with your team this week:

STEP 1: PICK A COMMON TREATMENT SCENARIO.

Choose something your practice sees regularly:

- Extraction + bone graft + membrane
- Crown and build-up
- Scaling and root planing (deep cleaning)
- Implant consultation

STEP 2: ASSIGN ROLES.

One person plays the patient. One person plays the treatment coordinator or presenter. Everyone else observes.

STEP 3: WALK THROUGH ALL SIX LAYERS.

The presenter should hit each layer in order:

- B: Start with bonding conversation
- A: Clarify the treatment and check understanding
- G: Explain insurance simply
- E: Ease into scheduling first
- L: Lock in payment options
- S: Secure some form of commitment

STEP 4: DEBRIEF AS A TEAM.

After each role-play, discuss:

- Did the patient feel rushed?
- Was anything confusing?
- Where did trust feel strongest—or weakest?
- Which layer felt most awkward or was skipped?

I still do this with my team today. I love watching them role-play, figure things out, and build confidence right in front of me. Usually, I let them play it out first—then I step in and say, "That was great... but now what if the patient says this instead?"

Because after years of sitting across from real patients, I've heard every excuse under the sun for why someone "can't move forward right now."

THE EXCUSES (AND WHAT THEY REALLY MEAN)

Once your team gets comfortable with the basic role-play—walking through the six layers with a cooperative "patient"—it's time to make things more realistic. Because in the real world, patients don't just nod along and say yes at the end. They push back. They hesitate. They throw out objections that seem to come from nowhere.

After years of patient conversations, I've heard every excuse under the sun. When I'm coaching my team through role-plays, I love throwing these curveballs at them.

Here are some of the greatest hits:

- "I need to check with my spouse." (Even though they came alone, for a cleaning, six months ago too, and the treatment plan was the same back then...)
- "I have to work that day." (And every other day you suggest, somehow.)
- "I'm redoing my kitchen." (Because granite countertops obviously come before saving your teeth.)
- "I'm going on vacation." (In six months.)
- "I just bought a boat." (Actual true story.)
- "I need to fix the roof first." (Even though it's sunny and 70 all week.)
- "I just got a new puppy and he's very expensive." (Valid... but still.)

Here's the truth: it's never really about the roof, the boat, the puppy, or the spouse. It's about fear. It's about trust. It's about needing a little more clarity—and a little more confidence.

When a patient throws out an excuse like these, they're not lying to you. They're telling you, in the only way they know how, that something in the conversation didn't land. They're not ready to say yes, and they're giving you a socially acceptable reason to end the conversation.

Your job isn't to argue with the excuse or push past it aggressively. Your job is to recognize it for what it is—a signal that you need to backtrack to an earlier layer. Maybe they need more bonding. Maybe they need better clarity on what the treatment involves. Maybe they need to understand their insurance better. Maybe they need payment options you haven't offered yet.

The best teams aren't the ones who say it perfectly the first time. They're the ones who know how to pivot with empathy, humor, and patience—and keep the conversation moving toward a yes without making the patient feel pressured or judged.

HANDLING COMMON OBJECTIONS: THE PIVOT APPROACH

When a patient gives you an excuse, don't argue. Acknowledge, explore, and redirect. Every objection is an opportunity to provide more clarity, more trust, or more options. Meet resistance with curiosity, not pressure.

"I need to check with my spouse."

"Absolutely, that makes sense for a decision like this. Would it help if I put together something you could share with them? Sometimes having the details written out makes that conversation easier."

"I need to think about it."

"Of course—it's a big decision. What questions can I answer that might help you think it through? I want to make sure you have everything you need."

"I can't afford it right now."

"I hear you. Let me show you some options that might make this more manageable. A lot of patients don't realize we can break this into payments. What monthly amount would feel comfortable?"

"I'm too busy to schedule."

"I get it—life is hectic. Let's look at what we have a few weeks out. Sometimes having it on the calendar actually makes it easier to plan around."

MAKING IT YOURS

The Bagel Method isn't meant to be a rigid script. It's a framework—a structure that guides your conversations while leaving room for your personality, your patient's needs, and the unpredictable moments that make every interaction unique.

Role-play in your morning huddles. Laugh at the absurd excuses patients give. Celebrate when someone nails a difficult case presentation. Build a culture where your team feels safe to try, fail, and improve.

When your whole team speaks the same language, something remarkable happens: case acceptance stops feeling like a battle and starts feeling like service. You're not convincing patients to do something they don't want. You're guiding them toward decisions that improve their health and their lives.

That's not sales. That's care.

Next, in Chapter 16, I'll share how all of these lessons—the systems, the culture-building, the case acceptance breakthroughs—led me to build something bigger than one practice. When you master your craft quietly behind the scenes long enough, eventually the world asks you to step into the spotlight.

Which layer of the Bagel Method feels the most awkward, rushed, or frequently skipped in your practice? How could role-playing with your team help strengthen that weaker area this month? And think back to a recent "let me think about it" patient: what excuse did they give, and what layer might have been missing from that conversation?

CHAPTER 16

STARTING YOUR COMMUNITY

When you master your craft quietly behind the scenes long enough, eventually the world asks you to step into the spotlight.

I didn't set out to build a community. I didn't plan to start a platform. I was just focused on doing my job better every day, earning trust with patients, creating systems for my practice, and developing stronger teams through real leadership. The spotlight was the last thing on my mind.

But as I mentioned back in Chapter 10, sometimes you don't find the stage—you look up and realize you've been building it all along. The expertise I was developing in insurance and coding and case acceptance was laying the foundation for something I couldn't yet see.

And the better I got at it, the more I realized something important. There were thousands of other managers out there just like me. Smart. Hardworking. Invisible. Trying to hold their offices together without enough support or recognition. Fighting the same battles I had fought, making the same mistakes I had made, feeling the same loneliness I had felt.

And I kept thinking: What if they didn't have to figure it out alone like I did? What if there was a place where managers could learn, grow, vent, connect, and get better together?

HOW DOMC STARTED (AND WHY IT MATTERED)

The Dental Office Managers Community didn't happen overnight. It started small—so small that calling it a "community" would have been generous.

Around the same time I became editorial director for DentistryIQ, I started a little Facebook group called Dental Office Managers. The first of its kind—an online home built for office managers, by an office manager. Not dentists. Not consultants. Not vendors. Just us.

I didn't create it because I wanted a title or a following. I created it because I needed a place to have the conversations no one else was having. How do you deal with burnout at the front desk? How do you actually talk to a patient about a $5,000 treatment plan without sounding pushy? How do you lead a team when you feel stuck in the middle between staff and doctors? How do you handle it when the doctor undermines you in front of patients?

I knew if I had these questions, other managers did too. At first, it was just a few conversations. A few posts. A few managers leaning on each other when no one else really understood what we carried day to day. There was no marketing plan. No growth strategy. Just a genuine desire to create connection. But because it was built on real need—because it was authentic, not manufactured—it grew.

I spent countless hours behind the scenes approving content, answering questions, moderating discussions, and jumping in when someone was having a hard day or needed encouragement. There was no paycheck for any of it, and no public applause. Just the quiet work of showing up consistently for people who needed what I had learned the hard way.

And somewhere along the way, it wasn't my group anymore. It became our community.

> 🧠 ***Manager Musings***
>
> *"You may not see it at first, but every hour you spend serving others is also building you."*

THE LONELINESS THAT CONNECTS US

We don't talk about it often, but dental management—really, any kind of middle management—can be lonely work.

You're not quite part of the clinical team. You're not the doctor. You're not corporate. You're somewhere in between—holding it all together, without always being recognized for it. You absorb stress from every direction. You solve problems no one knows existed. You carry weight that doesn't show up in any job description.

When you find even one other person who gets it, it feels like oxygen. That's what building a community gave me—and what it gave thousands of others, too. A place to be heard. A place to ask questions without fear of judgment. A place where you didn't have to explain yourself, because everyone already understood.

I remember the first time someone messaged me and said, "Thank you. I felt like I was the only one until I found this group." I stopped and read it three times. Because I remembered needing that feeling too. I remembered the isolation of those early years, wondering if everyone else had it figured out while I was barely keeping my head above water.

That kind of belonging changes your whole outlook and, subsequently, improves your work. When you know you're not alone—when you have people you can turn to who truly understand—you show up differently. You lead with more confidence. You take risks you wouldn't take in isolation. You become the manager you didn't know you could be.

REAL WINS FROM THE COMMUNITY

Building a community changed my career, because it showed me what becomes possible when people find each other. I've watched managers find their voices after years of being overlooked. I've seen front desk assistants rise into office manager roles, armed with systems and strategies they learned from the group. I've watched case acceptance rates climb as people implemented frameworks we discussed together. I've seen loneliness transform into leadership.

There was Sarah in Texas, who almost walked away from dentistry entirely. She was burned out, undervalued, and ready to quit. Instead, she found the community, connected with people who understood, and rebuilt her practice's systems using what she learned. She's still in dentistry today—and thriving.

There was Jen in California, who negotiated a major raise after the community helped her recognize her true value. She'd been underpaid for years, convinced she couldn't ask for more. After seeing other managers share their wins and their negotiation strategies, she made her case—and got what she deserved. Now she mentors others facing the same challenge.

That's what happens when you create a space where people belong. The collective wisdom becomes exponentially more valuable than anything one person could offer. Every question asked helps someone else who was too afraid to ask. Every success story inspires someone who thought success wasn't possible for them.

FROM MANAGER TO MENTOR TO MOVEMENT

Again, I didn't start the Dental Office Managers Community because I wanted to be famous. I started it because I knew there were others like me—people who were passionate, over-looked, and tired of feeling like they were doing it all alone.

Believe it or not, that's how most movements begin—not with ego, but with empathy. If you've ever solved a problem that used to overwhelm you, if you've ever helped a coworker get through something hard, if you've ever said, "There has to be a better way"—and then built it—you have the foundation for something bigger.

It doesn't have to look like what I built. Your version might be a study club, a social media page, a blog, a newsletter, a podcast, or an online course. It could simply be becoming the go-to mentor in your local professional network. The platform matters less than the purpose behind it.

Whatever form it takes, I urge you to start. Because there are people out there right now who need exactly what you've lived.

BUILDING YOUR PLATFORM: WHERE TO START

You don't need to build a massive community to make an impact. Start with what feels natural and sustainable.

Low Commitment: Share insights on LinkedIn, answer questions in existing groups, mentor one person, create a simple resource document.

Medium Commitment: Start a local study club, launch a newsletter, create a blog, offer to present at local events.

Higher Commitment: Build a dedicated online community, develop a course, start a podcast, write a book.

Ask yourself: What problem do you solve that others struggle with? What do people already ask you for help with? What would have helped you five years ago?

YOU DON'T NEED PERMISSION—YOU NEED PURPOSE

Nobody gave me permission to lead on a larger scale. Nobody certified me as qualified to start a community. I just had a reason that mattered, a willingness to serve, and the courage to be seen.

Big things don't come from perfect plans. They come from imperfect people who start anyway.

When you create something real, people notice. They come, they stay, and they bring others. And with that attention comes responsibility—to protect the culture, honor the mission, and keep it real no matter how big it gets.

The goal isn't scale. It's impact.

This chapter isn't really about how to start a movement. It's a reminder: sometimes the thing you build out of survival, out of service, out of empathy—becomes the thing that changes lives. Including your own.

WHEN COMMUNITY BECAME RESPONSIBILITY

There came a point—I couldn't tell you exactly when—where what had started as a space for connection started to feel like something heavier. The group wasn't just a place I'd created anymore. It was a place people counted on. Managers were making decisions based on conversations happening there. They were finding jobs, solving crises, getting through days they didn't think they could get through.

Somewhere in that shift, I realized the community wasn't mine to walk away from. Not because anyone demanded that of me, but because I'd built something that mattered to people beyond myself. That's a weight you don't expect when you start. But it's also a privilege you learn to carry.

FROM A GROUP TO AN ORGANIZATION

When I first started the Dental Office Managers Community, I wasn't trying to build a brand, a business, or an organization. I was simply trying to make sure office managers didn't feel as alone as I did.

At that point in my career, I had spent years being the person everyone relied on inside the practice—the fixer, the mediator, the one expected to have answers no one ever taught me. I knew there were thousands of office managers carrying the same weight, navigating the same pressure, and silently wondering if they were the only ones struggling.

The Facebook group started simply. A place to ask questions. A place to vent. A place to learn from others who actually understood the job.

What surprised me wasn't the growth—it was the depth of the need.

Managers weren't just looking for advice. They were looking for structure. Training. Validation. Confidence. They wanted to know what "good" actually looked like in their role, because most had been promoted without preparation and expected to figure it out on the fly.

Over time, the community became something bigger than a discussion space. It became clear that no single solution could support every office manager at every stage of their career. Some needed education. Some needed connection. Some needed leadership development. Others were ready to teach, speak, and influence the profession themselves.

That realization is what led to the creation of DOMA—the Dental Office Managers Alliance.

DOMA wasn't built as a program. It was built as an ecosystem—designed to meet office managers where they are and support where they're going next.

THE DOMA ECOSYSTEM

DOMA exists because dental office managers don't all need the same thing at the same time.

Throughout my career, I noticed something important: growth happens in layers. What helps you survive your first year in management isn't what helps you scale, lead, or create long-term fulfillment later on. Instead of building one solution, we built several—each serving a distinct purpose within the same mission.

DOMA MEMBERSHIP—THE EDUCATION FOUNDATION

DOMA Membership is the core educational layer of the ecosystem, designed for office managers who want clarity, confidence, and structure in their role—especially those who were promoted without formal training.

Membership focuses on leadership fundamentals, communication and accountability, case acceptance frameworks, systems and workflows, delegation and documentation, and operational confidence.

This is where survival turns into stability. For many managers, membership is the first time their role has ever been clearly defined—not by a job description, but by real-world expectations and proven systems.

DOMA LIVE EVENTS—CONNECTION AND IMPLEMENTATION

While education can begin online, some growth only happens in person. That's why DOMA includes two types of live events.

DOMA Pop-Up Events are free, two-hour gatherings typically held following major dental conferences. They're designed for relationship building, community connection, shared conversation, and practical leadership education. Pop-Ups give managers the opportunity to meet others who truly understand their role—often for the first time. They remove hierarchy and replace it with belonging.

DOMA Academy Live events are immersive, paid, full-day trainings focused on advanced leadership development, hands-on systems training, real-world implementation, and guided problem solving. Academy Live was created for managers who are ready to move beyond theory and into execution—applying what they've learned with clarity and accountability.

DOMA INFLUENCE ALLIANCE (DIA)

As DOMA continued to grow, another need became clear. Many of the strongest educators, consultants, and speakers in dentistry lacked visibility—while others had visibility without accountability or alignment.

The DOMA Influence Alliance was created to solve that gap. DIA is a vetted network of speakers, consultants, and educators aligned with DOMA's values of ethical leadership, real-world experience, and practical education.

Its mission is to elevate trusted voices, protect intellectual property, establish quality education standards, connect practices with proven experts, and support professionals ready to teach and lead. DIA ensures that education within the DOMA ecosystem is not only accessible—but credible.

ONE MISSION. MULTIPLE PATHS.

Some managers come to DOMA for education. Some come for community. Some come for leadership growth. Some come ready to influence the profession.

The ecosystem allows each individual to engage at the level that fits their season—without pressure, without hierarchy, and without losing the sense of belonging that started it all.

DOMA is not about creating noise in dentistry. It's about building a clear path forward—one that didn't exist when I needed it most.

> ### 🧠 *Manager Musings*
>
> *"You don't need to build an empire. Just a room where people feel like they belong."*

Building a community taught me that leadership isn't about titles or positions. It's about showing up—first for yourself, and then for others. And sometimes, when you show up consistently enough, opportunity finds you.

That's exactly what happened next. Not because I chased it. But because I lived it. And one day, someone asked me to bring my story to a bigger room.

Next, in Chapter 17, I'll share what happened when I said yes to an opportunity I didn't feel ready for—how I went from the back office to the keynote stage, and what I learned about the power of owning your story.

JOURNAL PROMPT

What kind of support would you have wanted earlier in your career—the space you wished existed when you were struggling? How could you create that feeling for someone else now? And ask yourself: what's stopping you from starting something, even small, that could help others who are where you used to be?

CHAPTER 17

TAKING THE STAGE

You never know who's watching while you're doing the work. But when the spotlight hits, you'll be ready—because you already lived it.

Remember back in Chapter 10, when the periodontist asked if I'd ever thought about speaking? That question planted a seed. I didn't tend to it consciously—I just kept doing the work. And eventually, that seed turned into something bigger.

One day, he asked me again. "You've got something to share, Kyle. Come speak next to me. On stage." Something I've learned in this career: when opportunity shows up, you show up too. So I said yes. And that one "yes" changed the entire course of my career.

SAYING YES BEFORE I FELT READY

The invitation felt like standing on a cliff's edge. Did I feel prepared? No. Was I nervous? Absolutely. The thought of standing in front of dental professionals who might know more than me, who might judge me—was terrifying.

But I knew something deeper. I had lived the kind of lessons that couldn't be Googled. I hadn't learned this stuff from textbooks. I had learned it from twenty years of showing up every day and figuring things out when there was no manual.

I didn't have a polished speaker bio or credentials designed to impress. What I had was a perspective that was earned, not borrowed. There's a difference between feeling ready and being ready. I wasn't confident, but I was credible. Sometimes that's enough to take the leap.

When I stood on that stage for the first time, everything I had ever gone through came with me. The early recall calls. The bagel lunches. The three-hour root canals for $200 insurance checks. The system breakdowns. The team rebuilds. The difficult conversations. The wins that nobody celebrated and the failures that kept me up at night.

THE "READY ENOUGH" FRAMEWORK

You'll never feel fully prepared for a bigger opportunity. Here's how to know when you're ready enough.

You're Ready Enough If:

- You've solved problems in this area that others still struggle with
- People already ask you for advice on this topic
- You have real experience, not just theories
- The opportunity scares you but also excites you

The Mindset Shift: Stop asking "Am I ready?" and start asking "Am I ready enough to add value?" Perfect readiness is a myth.

THE FIRST TIME I SAW MY STORY RESONATE

I remember my first talk clearly. I spoke on what I knew best: dental insurance coding and real-world case presentation. Nothing fancy.

I told stories from the front lines. I spoke about the headaches of dealing with insurance companies—the denials that made no sense, the appeals that took forever, the coding nuances that could mean the difference between getting paid and writing off hundreds of dollars. I shared how it really feels to be the invisible engine behind a practice, carrying weight that doesn't show up on any org chart.

When I finished, I expected polite applause. Maybe a few quick thank-yous as people filtered out to the next session. That's what happens at conferences, right? People clap, grab their things, and move on. Instead, people lined up. They asked questions—real questions, not the polite kind. They took notes. And that's when it hit me; this wasn't just about speaking—it was about representation.

I wasn't up there for me. I was up there for every office manager who had ever felt overlooked, overworked, and underestimated. For every person who had wondered if their struggles were unique or if everyone else had it figured out. For everyone who needed to hear that their experience mattered—that the hard-won lessons from the front desk were just as valuable as anything taught in dental school.

The audience didn't connect because I had perfect slides. They connected because I was telling their story, too—giving voice to experiences they'd never heard articulated on a stage before.

OWNING MY STORY, NOT JUST SHARING TIPS

The more I spoke, the more confident I became—not in my "presentation skills," but in the power of my perspective.

Because the truth is, there are plenty of people in dentistry who can tell you what the manual says. They can quote the CDT codes, recite the insurance regulations, walk you through the theoretical best practices. But very few can tell you what to do when a patient flips out at the front desk. How to ask for payment without sounding like a debt collector. How to rebuild trust after a toxic team member leaves. How to turn a broken, chaotic office into a fully functioning machine.

That's what I had. Not only theory, but lived experience. That's what connected with people. And that's what started to shift the way the industry saw dental office managers—not just as "support staff" but as leaders in their own right. Every time I took a stage, I was making a small argument that our perspective mattered. That the view from the front desk was valuable. That the people who kept practices running deserved to be heard, not just managed.

FROM SPEAKING TO LEADING WITH PURPOSE

Today, speaking is part of my life. But it's still personal.

I don't speak for applause or to build my brand. I speak to pour into the people who keep these practices running. The managers who haven't had a real vacation in two years. The new team lead who wonders if she's good enough.

I speak because I've lived it. And I want others to know: your experience matters. Your work matters. Your voice deserves to be heard. The stage doesn't scare me anymore—it grounds me. Because it's not about standing above. It's about standing with.

Since 2015, I've had the privilege of speaking at venues I never could have imagined when I was splitting bagels for lunch—from the Pennsylvania Dental Association to the California Dental Association, from dental schools to national conferences like Intellicon and The Dental Festival.

What surprised me was how often people asked for more. After presentations, after online conversations, managers kept saying the same thing: We want more time together. We want to keep learning. We want to actually meet each other.

That's what led to DOMA's live events—built around what managers kept telling me they needed. I didn't plan any of it. I just listened.

Each opportunity has been different—different audiences, different topics, different formats. But the message stays the same: Office managers are leaders. And it's time the industry treats them that way.

THE JOURNEY FROM INVISIBLE TO INFLUENTIAL

What started behind the front desk turned into a seat on the stage.

But here's what I want you to understand: the path from invisible to influential isn't about becoming someone different. It's about becoming more fully yourself—and then having the courage to share that self with others.

I didn't transform into a "speaker." I just started saying out loud what I'd been living quietly for years. The lessons were already there. Speaking just gave me a vehicle to share them.

You have that same raw material. Every challenge you've navigated, every system you've built, every crisis you've survived—it's all value. It's all something that could help someone a few steps behind you on the path.

WHAT THE STAGE TAUGHT ME

Standing on stages has taught me things I couldn't have learned any other way.

It taught me that authenticity beats polish every time. Audiences can smell rehearsed corporate-speak from a mile away. What they crave is honesty—someone willing to share not just their wins but their struggles.

And it taught me that representation matters more than I realized. When people see someone "like them" on a stage, it shifts their sense of what's possible. Every time an office manager takes a platform traditionally reserved for dentists and consultants, it expands what other managers believe they can become.

The stage is just a platform. What matters is what you do with it—and whether you use it to serve others or just to elevate yourself.

Next, in Chapter 18, I'll share what it looks like to create the career you weren't handed—because nobody is going to walk into your office and give you permission to lead bigger. You have to choose yourself.

JOURNAL PROMPT

Is there an opportunity right now that feels "too big" or "out of reach" for you? What would happen if you said yes—even before you felt fully ready? What's one small step you could take this month to step into a bigger version of yourself?

CREATING THE CAREER YOU WEREN'T HANDED

No one handed me a roadmap. So I drew one.
And now I'm handing the pen to you.

You've heard my story. But this book isn't about where I've been—it's about where you're going.

If there's one thing I've learned, it's this: the career you're dreaming about won't be handed to you. No one is going to walk into your office and say, "Hey—you've got leadership potential. Let's get you a raise and a speaking gig." That's never how it's worked.

You don't have to be chosen. You can choose yourself.

START BUILDING

Everything I've created—the practice turnarounds, the community, the events, this book—none of it came from being "tapped" out of nowhere. People like Mary and the periodontist opened doors for me. But they only opened those doors because I had already proven myself through the work.

The opportunities came because the work came first.

If you're reading this book, chances are you've been through some things too. You've survived difficult doctors, toxic coworkers, impossible patients. You've figured out systems nobody taught you. You've held things together when everything was falling apart.

That's your power. The experience is already banked. The credibility is already earned.

The rest? It's just reps. Courage. Action. And the willingness to say: "I don't need someone else to hand me a career. I can create one."

> 🧠 ***Manager Musings***
>
> *"The door might not be open for you yet, but that doesn't mean you don't belong in the room."*

THE PERMISSION TRAP

Most people stay stuck not because they lack talent or experience, but because they're waiting for permission that's never going to come.

They're waiting for their boss to suggest they apply for the promotion. They're waiting for someone to invite them to share their expertise. They're waiting for the "right time" when they'll finally feel qualified enough, confident enough, ready enough.

But that moment doesn't exist. There's always a reason to wait. The practice is too busy. The kids are at a difficult age. You need just a little more experience, a little more confidence. But "later" has a way of becoming "never."

Permission isn't something that gets granted from the outside. It's something you claim from the inside.

I didn't wait for PennWell Corporation to discover me—I pitched myself. I didn't wait for someone to start a community for office managers—I started one. Every step forward in my career came from betting on myself before anyone else did.

I started the Facebook group without a business plan, without knowing if anyone would join. I said yes to speaking before I had any idea what I was doing on a stage. Every significant thing I've built started before I felt ready. Readiness isn't something you feel—it's something you create through action.

YOUR CAREER WON'T LOOK LIKE MINE—AND IT SHOULDN'T

I'm not suggesting you follow my exact path. You don't have to start a community, speak at conferences, or write a book. Your version of "more" might look completely different from mine. And it should.

Maybe it's finally asking for the raise you deserve. Maybe it's taking on the leadership role you've been tiptoeing around—the one that scares you because you're not sure you're ready. Maybe it's mentoring the new hire instead of just training them. Maybe it's applying for the job you keep telling yourself is out of reach.

Whatever it is, move toward it. Stop circling. And if it scares you? Even better. That's usually the path.

THE CAREER CREATION FRAMEWORK

Careers aren't given. They're built one decision at a time.

Audit Your Assets: What have you learned that others haven't? What do people already come to you for? This is your foundation.

Identify Your "More": What does the next level look like for you? More money? More impact? More autonomy? Get specific.

Find the Gap: What's standing between where you are and where you want to be? A skill? A relationship? A fear? A conversation?

THE CAREER I CREATED (THAT YOU CAN TOO)

I started out doing recall calls on a wired phone with a bagel split into breakfast and lunch, making less than it cost me to commute. Now, I'm writing this book, still managing a thriving practice, leading events across the country, speaking for major dental organizations, and mentoring managers who are now building careers of their own.

The distance between those two points—the recall calls and the keynote stages—isn't talent. It's not luck. It's not connections I was born with or doors that were opened for me. It's relentlessness. It's showing up again and again, even when no one was watching. It's saying yes to opportunities that scared me. It's building things without knowing if they'd work. It's failing, learning, adjusting, and refusing to stay down.

You can do the same thing. Not my version of it, but your version. I hope this book gives you the signal that the path exists, even when you can't see it clearly. A signal that people who started where you are have gotten to where you want to be. A signal that your experience isn't a dead end—it's a launchpad.

If you feel like you've outgrown your current title, if you know you were meant to lead on a bigger level, or if you've been hoping someone will believe in you, then start by believing in yourself. That's where it all begins.

WHEN TO MOVE (EVEN IF YOU DON'T FEEL READY)

Move when you've been "thinking about it" for more than six months. When the fear of staying the same outweighs the fear of change. When you have enough experience to add value, even if not to be perfect.

Ask yourself: "If I don't make this move in the next year, how will I feel?" If the answer is "relieved," wait. If the answer is "regretful," it's time.

WRITING YOUR OWN JOB DESCRIPTION

When I started writing for DentistryIQ, there wasn't a role waiting for me. I saw a need and made myself useful. When I started the Facebook group, nobody was asking for it. I saw a gap and filled it.

Some of the most meaningful parts of my career didn't come from applying for existing positions. They came from seeing what was missing and building it.

What's broken that you could fix? What's missing that you could create? The best careers aren't "found." They're invented by people who see gaps and have the courage to fill them.

THE COMPOUND EFFECT OF SMALL MOVES

Each article I wrote built credibility for the next one. Each speaking engagement led to another invitation. Each problem I solved became a lesson I could teach others.

None of these steps felt significant in the moment. Writing one article doesn't change your career. Helping one person doesn't build a community.

But do it consistently, over years, and the compound effect is remarkable. The small moves stack. The first step makes the second possible. And eventually you look back and realize you've traveled a distance you never could have covered in one leap.

> 🧠 ***Manager Musings***
>
> *"The future of your career isn't written yet. But the pen is already in your hand."*

WHAT'S YOUR NEXT "YES"?

I've shared my story not so you can replicate it, but so you can see what's possible.

The question now is: what's your next yes? What's the thing you've been circling around, telling yourself you'll do "someday"?

Maybe it's small—asking for feedback on your leadership. Maybe it's medium—putting together your case for a raise. Maybe it's big—applying for a job that feels like a stretch.

You don't need to have it all figured out. You just need to take the next step. The path reveals itself as you walk it, not before.

You've spent this book learning what I've learned over two decades. The systems. The leadership principles. The case acceptance frameworks. But all of that knowledge is useless if you don't apply it—if you don't bet on yourself the way I eventually learned to bet on myself.

This is your turn. Not someday. Now. What are you going to build?

Next, in Chapter 19, I'll share the leadership legacy I hope you take from this book—because at the end of the day, this isn't about becoming like me. It's about becoming fully, fearlessly you.

What's one bold move you've been putting off? What would it look like to stop waiting and finally say, "It's my turn"? Be specific: what's the first action you could take this week to move toward the career you want instead of the career you've settled for?

CHAPTER 19

YOUR LEADERSHIP LEGACY

This isn't about becoming like me. It's about becoming fully, fearlessly you.

If you've made it this far, thank you.

However you got here—whether you read every word or skimmed for what applied to your Monday morning—I'm glad you're here. This book was never about reading it the "right" way. It was about finding something useful. Something that makes you more confident in your leadership.

As we close, I want to leave you with the truths that have shaped me. The things I wish someone had told me twenty years ago, when I was making recall calls and wondering if this career would ever amount to anything.

YOU'RE ALREADY A LEADER (EVEN IF NO ONE'S SAID IT OUT LOUD YET)

Leadership isn't a title. It's not tied to a paycheck or a place on the org chart. It's not something that gets conferred upon you in a ceremony or added to your email signature.

Leadership is showing up every day when no one says thank you. It's handling conflict with grace when you'd rather avoid it entirely. It's finding solutions when everyone else is stuck in the problem. It's holding space for others, even when you're barely holding it together yourself.

If you've done those things—even once—you're leading. Maybe no one has recognized it. Maybe you feel like you're "just the office manager" or whatever reductive label gets slapped on your role.

But I see you. I know what you carry. And I know that what you do is leadership, regardless of what anyone calls it.

So let me be the one to finally say it out loud: You're already a leader. Start owning that. Not arrogantly. But with quiet confidence in the value you bring.

YOU DON'T NEED TO DO IT ALL TO MAKE AN IMPACT

I know what it's like to believe you have to do everything, fix everything, be everything. The weight of being the person everyone relies on. The exhaustion of carrying more than one person should carry.

But your impact isn't measured by how much you do—it's measured by how much you shift the people around you. A leader who does everything creates a team that does nothing.

You just have to be present, consistent, and willing to come back again tomorrow—even when today was hard. That's what leaves a mark. The steady presence that builds trust over time. The calm in the chaos that gives everyone else permission to breathe.

I spent too many years believing my value was tied to my output. It took me a long time to realize that the best thing I could do for my team was to build them up so they could do things without me. That's a different kind of impact. A sustainable kind.

THE MOMENTS THAT BUILD YOUR LEGACY

At the end of the day, people won't remember how clean your ledger was. They won't remember whether you hit every metric. They'll remember how you made them feel.

   OVERWORKED, UNDERPAID, UNSTOPPABLE

They'll remember how you made the new assistant feel on her first day. How you handled a tough patient without losing your cool. How you supported your team through burnout. Whether you cared about them as people or just as functions on an org chart.

That's your legacy. And it's not built in big moments. It's built in the small ones that accumulate over time. Every conversation is an opportunity to build trust or erode it. Every day is a chance to leave people better than you found them.

THE LEGACY AUDIT

Consider how you'll be remembered by the people you lead.

For your team: Do they feel seen and valued? Do they come to you with problems, or hide them? Are they growing under your leadership?

For yourself: Are you proud of how you lead? Are you becoming the leader you'd want to work for?

The question that matters: Ten years from now, what will people say about what it was like to work with you? Start living that answer today.

LEADERSHIP IS A DAILY PRACTICE

One of the most important things I've learned is that leadership isn't a destination. It's a daily choice. You don't become a leader once and then coast. You choose it every single day—in every interaction, every decision, every moment when you could take the easy path or the right path.

Some days you'll lead well. Other days you'll fall short. You'll lose your temper. You'll avoid the conversation you should have had. You'll be human.

That's okay. Leadership isn't about perfection. It's about direction. The best leaders I've known aren't the ones who never make mistakes. They're the ones who own their mistakes and keep going.

FROM MY HEART TO YOURS

I wrote this book because I wish I had it twenty years ago.

When I was making those recall calls, splitting bagels, wondering if anyone saw the work I was doing—I wish someone had handed me a book like this.

I wish someone had told me it's okay to start small. That waiting until you can see the whole staircase just keeps you standing at the bottom. That the messy, uncertain beginning wasn't a sign I was doing it wrong—it was proof I was doing it at all.

I wish someone had told me I wasn't invisible. That even when no one said thank you, my work was landing somewhere. Someone was watching. The impact I couldn't see was still real.

I wish someone had told me my work mattered. That the systems I was building, the culture I was protecting—all of it mattered more than I knew. That I wasn't "just" an office manager. I was the person who made everything else possible.

And I wish someone had told me I didn't need to wait to lead. That leadership wasn't something that would be granted to me someday—it was something I could step into right now. I wasted years waiting for an invitation that was never coming. I don't want you to make the same mistake.

This book is my way of handing you the playbook I never got. It's my way of saying what I needed to hear back then: I see you. I know it's hard. And you're not alone.

Whether you go on to lead a team of two or two hundred— whether you stay where you are or build something entirely new—just know this: you already have what it takes. The experience is there. The lessons are learned. The capability is real. The only question is whether you'll believe it enough to act on it.

THE INVITATION

So here's my invitation to you, as we close this journey together.

Choose yourself. Move in this imperfect moment. Live what you already know is true—don't wait for someone else to validate it.

> 🎨 *Manager Musings*
>
> *"You already have what it takes. Now go build something that lasts."*

The career you want isn't going to be handed to you. The impact you're meant to make isn't going to happen automatically. These things have to be built—one decision at a time, one day at a time.

The frameworks are here. The lessons are here. What you do with all of it is up to you.

In the final chapter, I'll share some practical tools and resources to help you continue this journey—frameworks you can reference, questions you can revisit, and ways to stay connected with a community of leaders who are building alongside you.

What kind of leader do you want to be remembered as? Not the title or the accomplishments—but how you made people feel, what you stood for, and what you built. Write it down. Then ask yourself: what's one thing you could do tomorrow to start becoming that person today?

CHAPTER 20

ONE MORE THING BEFORE YOU GO

We've covered a lot of ground together.

From recall calls and bagel lunches to leadership roles and keynote stages. From feeling invisible to building a community of thousands. From the kid in Queens who learned to hold things together to the manager writing this book, hoping it helps you hold things together too.

We've arrived at the end of these pages—but hopefully at the beginning of something new for you.

THE THREAD THAT RUNS THROUGH EVERYTHING

If there's one thread that runs through every chapter, it's this: you don't have to wait for permission to become who you're capable of becoming.

Nobody handed me a roadmap. Nobody tapped me on the shoulder and said I was ready. Every step forward came from deciding—often before I felt ready—that I was going to move anyway. That my doubts didn't get to make my decisions.

That's not a personality trait. It's a choice. And it's one you can make too.

THE QUESTION THAT CHANGES EVERYTHING

When I first got invited to speak, my first thought was: "Why me?"

I wasn't a dentist. I didn't have advanced degrees. I was just a guy who'd figured some things out through trial and error.

But then I reframed the question: "Why not me?"

I'd ask you the same thing. Why not you? You've survived what others haven't seen. You've solved problems that weren't in any manual. You've held things together when everything was falling apart.

That's not "just experience." That's expertise. That's the foundation for whatever you want to build next.

WHAT ALL OF THIS BECAME

Every struggle in my journey pointed toward the same truth: office managers don't fail because they lack talent. They struggle because they lack support.

DOMA exists to change that. So no manager has to figure leadership out alone. So education is accessible and community is real.

It's not my finish line. It's my contribution.

WHAT I HOPE YOU TAKE WITH YOU

As you close this book, I hope you take more than frameworks and tactics. Those matter, but they're just tools. What I really hope you take with you is a shift in how you see yourself and what's possible.

I hope you see that leadership isn't a title—it's showing up when it's hard, having the conversations nobody wants to have, building people up even when you're barely holding it together yourself. You're already doing that. Start owning it.

And I hope you see that your experience has value. Every challenge you've navigated, every system you've built, every crisis you've survived—it's something that could help someone a few steps behind you. That's not "just experience." That's expertise.

THE BOOK IS FINISHED. YOUR STORY ISN'T.

I wrote this book because I needed it once—and I know you might need it now. When I was grinding through those recall calls, I needed someone to tell me it was going to be okay. That the struggle had a purpose.

This book is my way of being that person for you.

But books end. What happens next is up to you. You can put this on a shelf and go back to the way things were. Or you can take one thing—just one thing—and act on it. Have the conversation you've been avoiding. Ask for the raise. Say yes to something that scares you.

The size of the step doesn't matter. What matters is that you take it.

> 🧠 ***Manager Musings***
>
> *"You've read my story. Now go write yours. And make it a good one."*

FROM MY DESK TO YOURS

If you're still reading, I want you to know: I'm proud of you. Not for finishing a book—but for choosing growth. For believing there's more out there for you.

I don't know exactly what comes next—for me or for you. I'm still figuring it out, still building, still learning. What I do know is that the work continues. If you want to stay connected, the doors are open at DentalOfficeManagers.com.

Whatever you build from here, I hope you build it with the same truth that's carried me: you don't need anyone's permission. You just need to start.

If the kid splitting bagels in a windowless office can end up here—writing this book, leading this community, standing on stages he never imagined—then whatever you're dreaming about is possible too.

This book isn't just my story. It's yours now too.

Go build something that lasts.

With heart,

Kyle Summerford

Some doors you think are closed for good. Then the phone rings, and you realize they were just waiting for the right moment to open again.

I didn't see it coming. That's the honest truth.

By the time I got that call, life had moved forward the way it always does. The years had filled themselves with growth, setbacks, rebuilding, and becoming. Dentistry had taken me places I never imagined when I first walked into that small office in Queens as a kid just trying to survive.

But some numbers you never forget.

When I saw that number on my phone, I knew exactly where it was from. It was the first dental practice I had ever worked in. The place where everything started. The place that shaped how I think, how I lead, and how I see systems instead of just problems.

I answered.

MARY RETURNS

Her voice hadn't changed. Calm. Grounded. Familiar. The same voice that once asked me questions that forced me to think deeper. The same voice that believed in me before I believed in myself. The same person who had quietly left food on my desk when she knew I was struggling, without ever making me feel small.

We hadn't spoken in years. Nearly two decades had passed since the last time I had walked those hallways.

She didn't waste time.

"Kyle," she said. "We need help."

Not panic. Not chaos. Just honesty.

She explained what had been happening inside the practice. The dentistry had changed. The tools had changed. The software had changed. The screens were newer and the technology was faster. But underneath all of it, something felt familiar in a way that wasn't entirely comfortable.

The same strain. The same dependency. The same invisible weight carried by the same few people. The systems had grown more complex, but not necessarily stronger.

Then she said something that stayed with me.

"We need to redesign how this place runs."

Not fix a problem. Not put out a fire. Redesign.

That word mattered. Because redesign means you're no longer trying to survive the day—you're trying to change the future.

She told me she wanted to understand what was happening in dentistry now. Not just management. Not just workflow. The next era. The shift she could feel but couldn't yet define. She wanted to learn, to adapt, and to build something stronger than what they had relied on before. And she asked if I would come back.

For a moment, I didn't answer.

My mind went back to where this all started—the small desk, the recall calls, the long days, the uncertainty, the bagels split between meals, the quiet determination to keep going even when nothing felt certain. I thought about how much of my life had been shaped inside those walls. How many lessons were learned there. How many patterns I first saw there.

And now, after all those years, I was being asked to return—not as the kid trying to figure things out, but as someone who could help rebuild what once built me.

I told her yes.

WHAT I FOUND WHEN I WALKED BACK IN

Walking back into that practice after so many years felt familiar and different at the same time. The layout had changed. The technology had changed. The pace had changed. But the deeper patterns—the ones you don't see on a screen—were still there.

Busy schedules masking structural gaps. People carrying systems instead of systems supporting people. Knowledge living in heads instead of inside processes.

The practice wasn't broken. But it was carrying invisible strain—the kind that doesn't show up until complexity grows faster than structure can support it.

That's when I realized something important.

Dentistry hadn't just evolved. It had crossed into a new level of complexity—one that could no longer be stabilized by effort alone. Hard work wasn't enough anymore. Experience alone wasn't enough anymore. The old way of managing could hold things together, but it could not build what was coming next.

Something bigger was changing.

THE BEGINNING OF WHAT
COMES NEXT

I had walked back in thinking I was going to help a practice. But what I didn't expect was how much that visit was going to reshape how I thought about everything that came next.

And that realization would begin a journey that reshaped how I understood leadership, systems, and the future of dental practices.

At the time, I believed I was returning to help Mary. What I didn't realize was that this moment marked the beginning of the next chapter of my own life—one that would lead into new ways of thinking and a transformation far beyond anything I had known inside dentistry up to that point.

That journey led me somewhere I hadn't anticipated. Into a conversation about artificial intelligence and what it actually means for the people running dental practices day to day. Not the hype version. Not the version where robots replace everyone and the future arrives overnight. The real version, where the right tools, applied the right way, can finally give office managers the kind of leverage that effort alone never could.

That's what the next book is about. And if you've ever felt like you were carrying more than any one person should have to carry, I think it's going to matter to you.

JOURNAL PROMPT

Close your eyes and picture yourself one year from now. What's different? What have you built? What conversations have you had? What did you stop waiting for? Now open your eyes and ask yourself: what's the first step toward becoming that person? Write it down. Then go do it.

DOMA MEMBERSHIP

Leadership education, systems training, and real-world tools for office managers ready to lead with confidence.

→ DentalOfficeManagers.com

DENTAL OFFICE MANAGERS COMMUNITY (DOMC)

Connect with thousands of office managers nationwide who understand exactly what you're going through.

→ Search Facebook Groups for "Dental Office Managers Community"

DOMA LIVE EVENTS

Pop-Up events for connection and Academy Live trainings for implementation—across the U.S.

→ DentalManagerEvents.com

DOMA INFLUENCE ALLIANCE (DIA)

A vetted network of speakers, consultants, and educators aligned with the mission of serving dental teams with integrity.

→ www.domainfluencealliance.com

DOWNLOAD FREE FORMS, TEMPLATES, AND SCRIPTS

Ready-to-use patient forms, insurance narratives, case presentation templates, and more.

→ DentalOfficeManagers.com

LEARN ABOUT BECOMING AN AI DRIVEN DENTAL LEADER

→ Dentalaistandard.com

LEARN THE BAGEL METHOD™

Master the full case presentation framework.

→ DentalOfficeManagers.com/bagel-method

1:1 COACHING

Personalized mentorship for managers ready to level up.

→ KyleSummerford.com

CONNECT ON SOCIAL MEDIA

Daily tips and strategies.

→ Facebook.com/KyleLSummerford
→ Instagram-ManagingWithKyle
→ LInkedIn- Kyle-Summerford
→ Youtube.com/@kylesummerford

Kyle L. Summerford didn't start at the top. He started on a land-line, cold-calling overdue patients in a cramped back office in Queens, New York—eating half a bagel for breakfast and saving the other half for lunch.

That was over 24 years ago.

Today, Kyle is the leading voice on artificial intelligence in dental practice management—a keynote speaker, educator, and founder of one of the most influential ecosystems in the dental industry. He is the founder of the Dental Office Managers Alliance (DOMA), the largest professional organization for dental office managers in the United States, with a community of more than 25,000 members nationwide. He is the co-founder of Traynar.ai, the AI-powered training plat-form built for dental teams, and the creator of The Dental AI Standard framework—a practical guide to implementing artificial intelligence inside real dental practices.

Kyle has spoken at stages across the country, been featured in Dental Economics, DentistryIQ, Dental Lifestyles Magazine, and other leading industry publications, and has spent two decades helping dental professionals lead with clarity, confidence, and purpose.

But before any of that—he was just an office manager trying to figure it out. And that is exactly why this book exists.

He lives by one belief: you don't need anyone's permission. You just need to start.

Connect with Kyle:

→ Email- Kyle@joindoma.com

Other ways to connect-

→ Kylesummerford.com

→ DentalOfficeManagers.com

→ DentalAIStandard.com